The STRESS Management Workbook

An action plan for taking control of your life and health

The STRESS Management Workbook

An action plan for
taking control of your
life and health

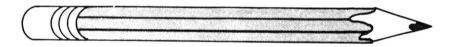

Stephen R. Aronson, PhD
Michael F. Mascia, MD, MPH

APPLETON · CENTURY · CROFTS / New York

81 82 83 84 85 86 / 10 9 8 7 6 5 4 3 2 1

Prentice-Hall International, Inc., *London*
Prentice-Hall of Australia, Pty. Ltd., *Sydney*
Prentice-Hall of India Private Limited, *New Delhi*
Prentice-Hall of Japan, Inc., *Tokyo*
Prentice-Hall of Southeast Asia (Pte.) Ltd., *Singapore*
Whitehall Books Ltd., *Wellington, New Zealand*

Library of Congress Cataloging in Publication Data

Aronson, Stephen R., 1943–   ; Mascia, Michael F., 1947–
    The stress management workbook.

    Bibliography: p.   1. Health.   2. Stress (Physiology)
3. Stress (Psychology)   4. Self-care, Health.   I. Title.
RA776.5.A76   613   81-8002
ISBN 0-8385-8696-1   AACR2

Design: Gloria J. Moyer

To our families

Contents

Preface xi
Acknowledgments xiii

1. Introduction to Stress 1
2. Signs and Symptoms of Stress 7
3. Identification of Stressors in Your Life 15
4. Increasing Stress Tolerance 123
5. Implementing Change 153

A Selected Bibliography 163

List of Charts, Exercises, Figures, and Questionnaires

Figure—An Integrated Model of Health and Disease ... 3
Figure—Cross Section of Integrated Model at Time X .. 4
Figure—Clinical Application of Integrated Model at
        Time X 5
Scale 1—Symptoms of Stress 8
Scale 2—Signs of Stress 12
Figure—Physical Stressors 16
Scale 3—Environmental Physical Stressors 17
Figure—Physical Supporters 19
Figure—Chemical Stressors 21
Scale 4—Environmental Chemical Stressors 23
Figure—Chemical Supporters 28
Figure—Biological Stressors 29
Scale 5—Environmental Biological Stressors 30
Figure—Biological Supporters 33
Figure—Social Stressors 34
Scale 6—Environmental Social Stressors 35
Figure—Social Supporters 37
Scale 7—Environmental Social Supporters 38
Figure—Attitudinal Stressors 40

Figure—Attitudinal Supporters 41
Scale 8—Attitudinal Stressors and Supporters 42
Scale 9—Self-Image Chart 45
Assessment Chart: The Need for Achievement 48
Assessment Chart: The Control Issue 52
Assessment Chart: The Workaholic Syndrome 54
Figure—Health Habits: Stressors 55
Scale 10—Health Habits: Stressors 56
Figure—Health Habits: Supporters 59
Scale 11—Health Habits: Supporters 60
Figure—Interpersonal Style: Stressors 63
Figure—Interpersonal Style: Supporters 63
Charting Your Support Network 64
Diagram—Diagramming Your Social Environment 66
Scale 12—Behavioral Stressors: Interpersonal Style ... 68
Figure—Behavioral Stressors 70
Figure—Behavioral Supporters 70
Scale 13—Internal Behavioral Stressors:
        Communication Skills 71
Diagram—Verbal Communication 74
Diagram—Nonverbal Communication 75
Confrontation Exercise 83
Problem-Solving Exercise 86
Anger Exercise 88
Responses to Anger 90
Strategies for Dealing with Anger 91
Expectations of Relationships 94
Approach to Decision Making 95
Scale 14—Social Stressors: Task-Based Stress 98
Scale 15—Social Stressors: Role-Based Stress 99
Changing Responsibilities 100
Role Problems 101
Eggs in Your Baskets 103
Scale 16—Social Stress: Situational Factors 104
Life Stage Exercise 107
The Social Readjustment Rating Scale 108
Figure—Genetic Stressors 110
Scale 17—Genetic Stressors 111
Figure—Genetic Supporters 114
Figure—Immunity 114
Figure—Immunological Stressors 115
Figure—Immunological Supporters 116
Immunization Chart 117

Scale 18—Immunization 118
Figure—Pathological Internal Conditions 119
Level of Pathology Questionnaire 120
Improving Stress Management Strategies: Pre-Test 123
Conditioning Questionnaire 124
Present Activities Chart 126
Future Activities Chart 128
Carbohydrate Consumption 130
Fat Consumption 134
Protein Consumption 136
Calculating Your Total Daily Protein Consumption 138
Vitamin Consumption 140
Future Food Consumption Instructions 143
Scale 19—Methods of Relaxation 144
Recreation and Hobbies 152
Checklist of Stressors and Supporters 153
Action Plan for Change 158
Support Network Help for Your Action Plan 160
Improving Stress Management Strategies: Post-Test ... 161

Preface

The twentieth century has been marked by tremendous advances in the theory and practice of medicine. Phenomenal scientific and technological discoveries have found their way into medical practice. People have grown to expect certain seemingly miraculous results from the institutions and providers of medical care, and often, the expectation is that the "impossible" can be achieved.

There is, however, increasing popular awareness that modern medicine cannot perform miracles despite the available science and technology. Professionals and laymen alike are learning that advances in medicine, however dazzling, cannot make up for life styles that breed pathology. Life style is now being recognized as a major factor in the development of many of our modern medical problems. General attitude and behavior are clearly linked to the individual's health status. Moreover, most medical problems seem to occur more frequently with increasing stress, and environmental exposure appears to be a factor in most illnesses. Expectations appear to have an effect on health and well-being. Such varied problems as cancer, cirrhosis of the liver, malnutrition, pancreatitis, ulcers, high blood pressure, headache, food poisoning, voodoo deaths, and others appear to be influenced by both internal and environmental factors, both emotional and physical.

Professionals and laymen are beginning to realize and teach that the individual has a great responsibility in the promotion of his own health and the prevention of his own disease. The concept of self-care is steadily gaining acceptance. People are beginning to realize that they have control over certain factors that affect their health and well-being. But although these concepts are being accepted more readily, the methods for their application and general use have not been widely available.

THE STRESS MANAGEMENT WORKBOOK is designed for the individual who takes the concept of self-care seriously and wants to do whatever he* can to promote his own health and well-being, as well as take advantage of the best that modern medicine has to offer.

Although the book can be read rather quickly, the material is designed to be implemented gradually and thoughtfully in conjunction with advice from your personal physician. It is expected that your initial planned changes may take up to two years or more to institute.

---

*Throughout the book we have used such constructions as "the individual . . . he" solely for the economy of language. Our usage of personal pronouns is not, in any way, intended to imply any connotation of sexual role discrimination.

Frequent review of the material should take place during this time, and modifications of the plan will not be uncommon. Modifications, again, should be placed into a reasonable timetable.

It is common for individuals to identify with many of the symptoms, behaviors, and attitudes discussed in this book. This is not cause for alarm. It does not necessarily mean that you have a serious problem; the information you gather will certainly help you to know yourself better and facilitate your personal growth.

This book has been designed for use as a self-help manual for the individual, as a text for students of healing professions as part of an in-house training program in a work setting, or as part of the *Stress Management Workshop,* which is conducted by the authors upon request. If it is being used in an employer-sponsored program, care should be taken to establish a degree of confidentiality that will facilitate honest responses to the material.

FOR THOSE USING THIS BOOK FOR INDUSTRIAL TRAINING:
A NOTE TO MANAGERS, SUPERVISORS, AND OTHER PEOPLE IN CHARGE OF PEOPLE

The people you manage are not likely to do all the work in this book nor are they likely to fill out the Action Plan for Change, much less follow through without your example and encouragement. If the health of those you supervise is important to you, if you believe that productivity will increase, that absenteeism and staff turnover will decrease with increases in your staff's ability to cope with stress, then it is your job as manager to establish conditions that encourage completion and follow through with this material.

1. Make it clear to staff that their cooperation with this project is part of their job and that they are expected to complete all the work in this book.

2. Build time into the schedules of your workers for them to complete this material.

3. Pay them to do this work if time is not made available in their work schedules.

4. Set up a series of ongoing interviews over the next one to three years, at least two to three per year of follow-up, to discuss their progress and encourage them to follow through.

5. Reward, either financially or through some type of recognition, those employees who meet their own goals for stress management and stress reduction.

6. Lastly, *if you do not set the example and demonstrate the importance of this program to the agency, business, or organization, your staff will not take it seriously. If you need help structuring and implementing this type of follow-up program, consult your company or personal physician and/or professional counselors/organizational consultants to help guide you through the process of change which you have found desirable.*

Acknowledgments

We wish to thank Cheryl Fuller-Aronson and Elizabeth Mascia for their valued suggestions and critical reading of our text; Robert Doyle, M.D., for his careful review and professional criticism of the material; Josie Hays for her patient and knowledgeable typing of the text; Donna Knightly for her detailed proofreading and comments; and Judy Barrington for her excellent artwork. Their contributions, all of which made writing THE STRESS MANAGEMENT WORKBOOK an easier task, are sincerely appreciated. A special thanks is owed to the editors of Appleton-Century-Crofts, especially Kate Brown whose precision and skills have been invaluable in the final preparation of the manuscript.

The STRESS Management Workbook

An action plan for
taking control of your
life and health

1
Introduction to Stress

Stress is frequently used today as a derogatory term referring to social and psychological factors that adversely affect modern man. For purposes of this book, however, stress is defined as any internal or environmental, real or imagined condition, event, or agent that elicits a physical or psychological response in a person. This is a very general biological definition of stress and is deliberately vague. The important aspect of the definition is that for a condition, event, or agent to be a stress, it *must* elicit a response in the person. No response means no stress. Each agent, event, or condition that has the ability to elicit a response in the organism is called a *stressor*. The effects of stress on the individual are determined by the magnitude of the stressor and the preexisting condition of the individual.

Stress is a normal part of our daily lives. We have all experienced varying degrees of stress during different times of our lives. The amount of stress that we experience varies from hour to hour, day to day, week to week, and year to year. And each of us reacts to stress in different ways. Each of us also has a different ability to deal with stress. It is true, however, that no matter how great our ability to cope with stress, we each have our limits. If we consistently exceed our limits of stress tolerance, loss of well-being and/or illness will result. The problem is that most of us have no idea how much stress we are tolerating, how much stress we are capable of tolerating, how we can reduce our stress load, and how we may increase our stress tolerance. Moreover, few of us realize that we have the power to control much of the stress in our lives. In this chapter, we will examine some of the basic research showing the relationship between health and stress, and we will provide you with a basic model that explains the relationship between stress and health and demonstrates which factors can be influenced or controlled.

The relationship between stress and health has been chronicled at least since the beginning of this century. In 1910, Sir William Osler pointed out the relationship between coronary chest pain and stress. In 1927, Walter Cannon published material indicating some details of the body's response to stress. He recognized a general discharge of the sympathetic nervous system as a preparatory bodily response to an actual or perceived threat to the individual. This response to maintain internal conditions of the body and prepare it for self-defense (for survival) was observed as a reaction to strong muscular exercise, asphyxia, hypoxia (low levels of oxygen in the blood), pain, emotional excitement, hypoglycemia (low blood sugar), and rage. In 1936, Hans Selye further defined this response to stress and termed it the *general adaptation syndrome.*

Since then, many researchers have defined the physiology of the body's response to stress. Current research indicates the body's response to stress is far more complicated than the early research indicated. Recent investigations by James Henry and Daniel Ely indicate at least two physiological response patterns to stress depending on the organism's perception of the stimulus. If the stress is a perceived *threat to control,* the general adaptation syndrome is elicited. If the stress is perceived as a *loss of control,* a depressive response (passive behavior, withdrawal) results. In 1958, Dr. Lawrence Hinkle and Dr. Harold Wolf, two industrial physicians, published material indicating an association between psychological stress and human disease. Their research was based on the data accumulated prospectively over a 20-year period. These two industrial physicians found that illness "peaked" every 7 years in American blue-collar workers and every 3 years in Chinese blue-collar workers. That means that illnesses occurred most frequently at these times. Illness peaks in both groups of workers corresponded to life circumstances that were considered *intolerable* and *unchangeable* by the individuals involved. Moreover, Hinkle and Wolf showed that a majority of illness occurred in a minority of the population being evaluated. Since the 1960s, Dr. Thomas Holmes has been publishing the results of his research, and much of his work has recently been popularized in the lay press as the Social Readjustment Scale. (This scale appears in Chapter 5.) His research allows quantification of psychosocial stress through use of a scale of life events and has shown that the likelihood of illness increases with increasing stress. Richard Rahe has demonstrated increased mortality from heart attacks (myocardial infarctions) with increased stress.

The research touched upon here is only a small part of the available, convincing information. In summary, research indicates that stress of sufficient quantity and duration contributes to an individual's ill health and lack of well-being. If the individual's preexisting condition is poor, serious illness or death may result. If the preexisting condition is good, lack of well-being or minor illness may result.

Stress is a confusing term. Its meaning is not clear even among those who have studied it closely. The researchers previously mentioned have selected their own definitions of stress, and the popular definition of the word varies with time. Common usage today defines stress as some "bad" environmental force that must be avoided at all costs. Stress becomes a problem when it adversely affects our ability to feel well and function normally. Abnormally prolonged or frequent response to stressors does appear to have adverse effects.* By the same token, minor responses to minor stresses in a debilitated person may be the final factor in causing a major illness. Are all responses detrimental? No, but all responses are potentially detrimental depending on the prior condition of the individual. The prior condition is determined by prior stress load and existing state of health. What is stressful and detrimental to you may be stressful and beneficial to another. Running (within limits) is stressful but beneficial for a healthy person, but it is potentially lethal for a person with coronary artery disease or congenital heart disease. A baseball game may be relaxing although

---

*Some people refer to these adverse effects as strain.

AN INTEGRATED MODEL OF HEALTH AND DISEASE

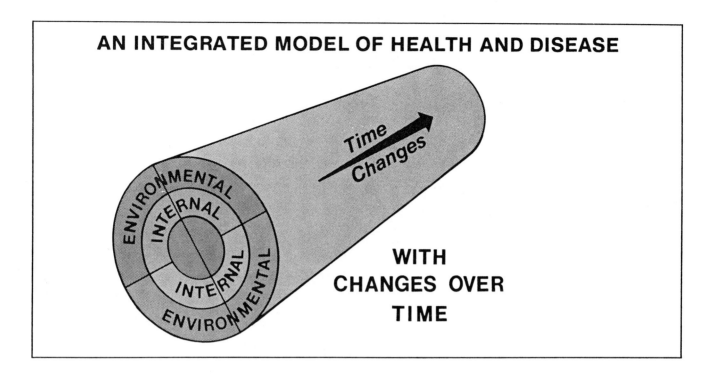

WITH CHANGES OVER TIME

stressful and exciting for a healthy person, but a grand slam home run can be a lethal dose of excitement for a coronary-prone individual.

Are you a person who can benefit from certain stressors but should avoid others? How can you change your attitude and behavior to improve your stress tolerance? How can you improve your attitude in order to reduce adverse stress? To explore these and other questions more fully, we have developed a theoretical model that incorporates many of the known stressful factors that impinge upon our lives (see the above figure).

The interaction of the individual with the environment determines that individual's overall functional ability and sometimes results in disease or pathology. Pathology in the individual may, in turn, result in a temporary or permanent reduction in functional ability.

As can be seen by examining the model, individuals are exposed to environmental and internal stressors and supporters. Some of the stressors are alterable and some are unalterable. These variables change over time, and their interaction determines an individual's overall stress tolerance and well-being at any given time. Internal pathology (disease or abnormality) plays a large role in determining stress tolerance. In this book, we will be discussing primarily alterable factors, factors that you can change to promote your health and well-being. The following figure gives examples of factors that can be affecting your health at any given time (see Figure 2).

The figure on page 5 represents how a real patient with pneumonia might look from the perspective of the Integrated Model. This person's stress tolerance would probably be low at this time. The expectation is that the patient would probably recover over time with or without treatment because of internal and environmental supporters. However, excessive stress on environmental support might be devastating;

There are three basic components of the Integrated Model: internal factors, environmental factors, and time. The interaction of the factors varies over time and determines the overall functional ability of the individual.

*It should be noted that certain "unalterable" environmental factors can be altered through industrial and/or governmental action, but usually not through individual behavioral change.

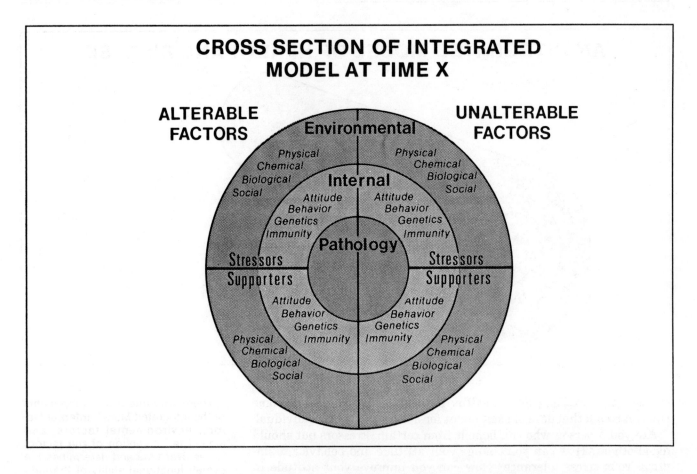

for example, withdrawal of family support during the delusions of a high fever might result in this person's injuring himself.

The individual's stress tolerance is limited. Psychosocial stress could result from loss of family support and might be devastating unless some other support system, such as a hospital, was available. Excessive or prolonged increased stress would be intolerable and could possibly result in death or permanent disability. This is just one example. We are all experiencing thousands of environmental and internal stressors and supporters at all times. Many of the alterable factors will be examined in more detail in the following chapters. The following analogy further explains the relationship between stressors and supporters and your level of functioning.

A pickup truck is designed to perform certain functions. It has built-in load-carrying limits, speed capabilities, engine rpm limits, and terrain limits. It must be maintained properly and must get proper fuel. If the design limits are exceeded without appropriate accommodating design changes, the vehicle will not function properly and may be damaged. A one-ton pickup truck can carry one and one-half tons for a short distance at slow speed over level ground, probably without damage. If the driver speeds on rough terrain with a heavy load, however, damage will probably result. If the truck has heavy-duty suspension installed, the load capacity may be doubled from one to two tons without damage on all reasonable road conditions and at all but excessive speeds.

Man is similar to this pickup truck. The load is the accumulation of his stressors; the design is his stress tolerance; and the suspension is the sum of his supporters. Man differs in that he must learn his own

CLINICAL APPLICATION OF INTEGRATED MODEL AT TIME X

ALTERABLE FACTORS

UNALTERABLE FACTORS

A

Physical:	temp. 100° F.
Chemical:	--------
Biological:	flu exposure risk high, pollen count high
Social:	--------

B

Attitude:	poor tolerance to illness
Behavior:	takes medicine poorly, workaholic
Genetics:	--------
Immunity:	--------

C

| Pathology: | pneumonia, temp. 104° F |

D

Attitude:	aggressive, helps self
Behavior:	eats well no tobacco
Genetics:	--------
Immunity:	fully immunized heals rapidly

E

Physical:	cool house, air conditioning, air filtered
Chemical:	good water
Biological:	on antibiotics, family and contacts healthy
Social:	physician treated, family supportive

F

Physical:	volcanic eruption, full moon, summer weather (hot, humid)
Chemical:	smog, ozone
Biological:	flu epidemic, plants in bloom, insects emerging
Social:	recent death of brother, high unemployment, high inflation

G

Attitude:	--------
Behavior:	--------
Genetics:	male, family history of hay fever
Immunity:	no history of immune problems

H

| Pathology: | age 30, congenital absence of kidney |

I

Attitude:	--------
Behavior:	--------
Genetics:	family history of longevity
Immunity:	--------

J

Physical:	changing weather front, changing moon phase, volcanic eruption expected to cease
Chemical:	air expected to clear
Biological:	flu epidemic on the wane
Social:	extended family with strong relationships

capacity to tolerate stress: His capacity changes with age, time, and attitude, and he must develop his own support system. In the chapters that follow, you will be taught how to increase your feeling of well-being and to reduce your chances of major illness by learning how to identify your excess stress, how to identify stressors, how to avoid excess stress, and how to increase your stress tolerance.

2
Signs and Symptoms of Stress

SYMPTOMS OF PSYCHOSOCIAL STRESS

Symptoms: *Unpleasant subjective feelings that correspond to physiological or bodily changes.*

LIST OF SYMPTOMS		
Palpitations	Decreased interest in sex	Thoughts or fears of failure
Chest pain	Insomnia	Irritability
Unexplained sweats	Loss of appetite	Jaw pain
Headache	Neck pain	Tooth pain
Abdominal pain	Back pain	Worry about being sick
Diarrhea	Fatigue	Tension
Constipation	Confusion	Repetitive thoughts
Aches and pains	Agitation	Trouble breathing
Increased interest in sex	Anxiety	Other

Symptoms are subjective feelings that correspond to physiological or bodily changes. Stressors may produce bodily responses that are not noticeable to the individual. In other words, a person may be under stress without symptoms. Also, a person may be under stress and be experiencing pleasure. That is, stress may be associated with no feelings, with unpleasant body sensations (symptoms), or with feelings of well-being (pleasure). Excess stress, however, is almost universally associated with unpleasant bodily sensations, that is, symptoms. Symptoms may also represent bodily changes corresponding to pathology or disease. The untrained individual is usually unable to differentiate between symptoms from stress and symptoms from disease.

Scale 1 which follows is a listing of symptoms that are commonly seen with psychosocial stress. Filling it out will accomplish two goals: Goal 1 is to allow you to identify symptoms that you usually experience when under psychosocial stress (column headed "Past Stressful Times"). This will enable you to build your individual profile. When you notice one of your stress symptoms, you can then recognize what is happening and work to change the situation. Goal 2 is to allow you to explore the extent to which you are *currently* under stress (column headed "Past Two Weeks").

SCALE 1–SYMPTOMS OF STRESS

For each of the listed symptoms, write in the number from 1 to 5 that approximates the extent to which you have experienced it. Comment or give examples to clarify your answers and write in "X" if you do not know. When in doubt, choose the higher number.

5	4	3	2	1	X
Daily	**Weekly**	**Monthly**	**Rarely**	**Never**	**Do Not Know**

PAST TWO WEEKS	PAST STRESSFUL TIMES	

A*_____ _____ **1.** Palpitations (pounding in chest, heart skipping)

Comment: _____

_____

A _____ _____ **2.** Chest pain

Comment: _____

_____

A _____ _____ **3.** Unexplained sweats

Comment: _____

_____

A _____ _____ **4.** Headache

Comment: _____

_____

A _____ _____ **5.** Abdominal pain

Comment: _____

_____

A _____ _____ **6.** Diarrhea

Comment: _____

_____

A _____ _____ **7.** Constipation

Comment: _____

_____

_____ _____ **8.** Increased or decreased interest in sex

Comment: _____

_____

*Code: A, active relaxation methods helpful; P, passive relaxation methods helpful. (See text for further explanation.)

5	4	3	2	1	X
Daily	**Weekly**	**Monthly**	**Rarely**	**Never**	**Do Not Know**
PAST TWO WEEKS	PAST STRESSFUL TIMES				

   _____   _____

9. Insomnia (sleeplessness)

Comment: _____

_____

   _____   _____

10. Loss of appetite

Comment: _____

_____

A _____   _____

11. Neck pain

Comment: _____

_____

A _____   _____

12. Back pain

Comment: _____

_____

   _____   _____

13. Fatigue

Comment: _____

_____

P _____   _____

14. Confusion

Comment: _____

_____

A _____   _____

15. Agitation

Comment: _____

_____

P _____   _____

16. Anxiety (worry)

Comment: _____

_____

P _____   _____

17. Keep thinking about a problem—can't get it out of your mind

Comment: _____

_____

A _____   _____

18. Trouble breathing

Comment: _____

_____

P _____   _____

19. Thoughts or fears of failure

Comment: _____

_____

continued

5	4	3	2	1	X
Daily	**Weekly**	**Monthly**	**Rarely**	**Never**	**Do Not Know**
PAST TWO WEEKS	PAST STRESSFUL TIMES				

————	————	**20.** Irritability
		Comment: _____
		_____
A ————	————	**21.** Aches and pains
		Comment: _____
A ————	————	**22.** Jaw pain
		Comment: _____
————	————	**23.** Tooth pain
		Comment: _____
————	————	**24.** Worry about being sick
		Comment: _____
A ————	————	**25.** Tension (tightness of muscles)
		Comment: _____
————	————	**26.** Other _____
————	————	_____
————	————	_____
————	————	_____
————	————	_____
————	————	_____
————	————	_____
————	————	_____
————	Totals	

Code: A, active relaxation methods helpful; P, passive relaxation methods helpful. (See text for further explanation.)

The higher your total, the more likely you are to be experiencing excess stress. The lower your total, the less likely you are to be experiencing excess stress. No absolute scores will be assigned to these scales to arbitrarily define "high" and "low." The scales are primarily guides to sensitize you to your symptoms of stress. You must evaluate yourself on the degree to which you believe that a given scale *may be* significant for you. Check with your physician if you even suspect you might have a problem. If your score is high and you have not seen a physician for evaluation of your symptoms, you should do so in order to exclude the possibility of serious illness. If serious illness has been excluded by your physician, there are several other approaches to relieving stress-induced symptoms. If you scored higher on numbers 1–7, 11, 12, 15, 18, 21, 22, and 25 (those marked "A"), you are more likely to benefit from some active form of relaxation, such as running, jogging, tennis, or some other form of exercise. If you had a predominance of high scores on numbers 14, 16, 17, and 19 (those marked "P"), you may be more likely to benefit from some passive form of relaxation, such as meditation, yoga, deep-muscle relaxation, or self-hypnosis. If you have a balance of the two types of symptoms, you may benefit more from a combination of the two forms of relaxation. (You may have noticed that not all the numbers have been listed in this review. The reason is that those particular symptoms are a mixed variety and do not tend to fall within either category.) If the symptoms you are experiencing are debilitating, persistent, or severe, check with your doctor to exclude serious illness or at least the possibility of a need for treatment.

SIGNS OF PSYCHOSOCIAL STRESS

Signs: *Objective or observable external evidence of internal, physiological change. Signs and symptoms sometimes go together to define a pathological condition or disease. However, some signs are usually representative of psychosocial stress and rarely indicate disease. A physician may have to make that determination.*

LIST OF SIGNS

Increased alcohol use	Changes in posture
Increased drug use	Hyperventilation
Increased tobacco use	Lack of control
Weight gain	Increased spending of money
Weight loss	Reckless behavior
Increased activity	Poor judgment
Reduced activity	Increased sexual activity
Pacing the floor	Reduced sexual activity
Wringing hands	Loss of effectiveness at work
Worried look	Increased eating
Throwing objects	Reduced eating
Kicking objects	Other
Slamming objects	

The following scale is designed to help measure your signs of stress. These signs are frequently seen with psychosocial stress and rarely represent disease. Please fill out the following form.

SCALE 2–SIGNS OF STRESS		
Please respond to the following statements.		
2	1	X
Yes	**No**	**Do Not Know**
PAST TWO WEEKS / **PAST STRESSFUL TIMES**		

I have or those around me have noticed:

_____   _____   **1.** I have gained or lost weight.

Comment: _____

_____

_____   _____   **2.** I have increased or reduced my physical activity.

Comment: _____

_____

_____   _____   **3.** I pace the floor.

Comment: _____

_____

_____   _____   **4.** I wring my hands.

Comment: _____

_____

_____   _____   **5.** I have a worried look.

Comment: _____

_____

_____   _____   **6.** I throw, kick, or slam objects.

Comment: _____

_____

_____   _____   **7.** I have changed my posture (for example, hanging head down, shuffling my feet, drooped shoulders).

Comment: _____

_____

_____   _____   **8.** I hyperventilate (rapid breathing).

Comment: _____

_____

_____   _____   **9.** I lack control (for example, yelling, intolerance, lack of patience, etc.).

Comment: _____

_____

continued

2	1	X
Yes	**No**	**Do Not Know**
PAST TWO WEEKS PAST STRESSFUL TIMES		

I have or those around me have noticed:

_____   _____   **10.** I have increased my drug use (e.g., alcohol, coffee, tea, tobacco, tranquilizers, sleeping pills, marijuana, etc.).

Comment: _____

_____

_____   _____   **11.** I have increased my spending of money.

Comment: _____

_____

_____   _____   **12.** My behavior seems reckless.

Comment: _____

_____

_____   _____   **13.** I have increased sexual desire.

Comment: _____

_____

_____   _____   **14.** I have reduced sexual desire.

Comment: _____

_____

_____   _____   **15.** I am less effective at work.

Comment: _____

_____

_____   _____   **16.** I have increased or reduced appetite.

Comment: _____

_____

_____   _____   **17.** I bite my fingernails.

Comment: _____

_____

_____   _____   **18.** Other _____

_____

_____   _____

_____   _____

_____   _____

_____   _____   Totals

The higher your score in the first column, the more likely you are to be under excess stress now. The higher your score in the second column, the more likely you were to have been reacting to excess stress at those particularly bad times you happen to remember. The lower your scores, the less likely you are to be experiencing or to have experienced excess stress. Remember, if your scores are high and you have not seen a doctor recently, you should check with your physician in order to exclude serious illness. If your scores are high and you do not have a serious illness, then you are likely to benefit from one of the many relaxation methods described in Chapter 4 in combination with a reduction of the stress load you are experiencing.

In any case, if the signs and symptoms are debilitating (exhausting), persistent, or severe, check with your doctor in order to exclude serious illness or the need for professional treatment.

3
Identification of Stressors in Your Life

ENVIRONMENTAL FACTORS

In this chapter, we will be examining some of the major sources of stress in today's world. As you will recall, any agent, event, or condition that has the ability to elicit a response in an individual is called a stressor. In other words, a stressor is anything in the individual or in his environment that causes a change or response in that individual. In addition to examining sources of stress, we will be examining sources of support within the individual and his environment. We will try to take as comprehensive a view as is possible.

Some people may feel overwhelmed by the recognition of their exposure to environmental hazards. For some people, quantification of personal exposure is an extremely frightening experience. The following series of exercises is not meant to be either frightening or overwhelming. Do not panic. The numbers are here to help you learn more about what you can do for yourself. They are not intended to predict early illness for you or your demise. You can use the numbers to define your problem areas and to make plans for gradual changes (over two years, more or less). The numbers are also useful for comparison: now versus the future. Do not give up on first glance; follow through with the explanations.

PHYSICAL STRESSORS	
Temperature	Work (physical)
Pressure	Inertia
Humidity	Gravity
Radiation	Microwave
Visible light	Radiowave
Ultraviolet light	Magnetism
Sound	Momentum
Particulate matter	Others
Electricity	

Physical Stressors

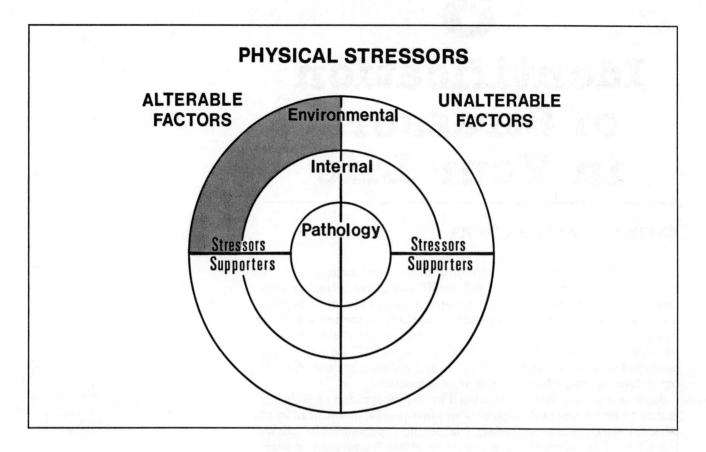

Physical Stressors: *Agents, conditions, or events to which you are potentially or actually exposed and that are known to have an adverse effect on man.*

Some of these factors are experienced by most of us on a daily basis. Most of us are exposed to moderate temperatures (40 to 80°F) and moderate *temperature changes*. However, extremes of temperature are not unusual, and they may be extremely stressful. *Changes in barometric pressure* are normal, but even standard changes seem to have significant effects on many people. Extremes in atmospheric pressure are extremely stressful and dangerous. *Radiation* (x-ray) exposure is limited in most natural environments. However, low-level radiation is found in some water supplies and occupational exposure is not uncommon. Nuclear waste is a potential problem. *Ultraviolet light* is part of the normal light spectrum, and we are all exposed to it daily when out in the sunlight. For some of us, especially those with fair skin, the long-term result of exposure may be cancer of the skin. The *length of day* (hours of light) affects circadian rhythm and wake-sleep patterns. *Trauma*—direct, sudden violence—is a normal part of daily living. However, as we all know, the more severe the trauma, the more significant the injury. The location of the trauma is also important in determining the significance of the injury. *Immersion,* or the placing of part or all of the body under water, tends to be a pleasant experience for most of us. However, when temperatures are very high or low or the length of time is prolonged or the person cannot remain above water, the stresses can be lethal. *Motion* at moderate speeds is usually pleasant or at least tolerable. However, rapid acceleration and/or extreme speed can have unusual effects. *Sound* of moderate intensity is a potentially pleasant experience. Extremely loud sound is unquestionably a destructive stressor both psychologically and physically. *Particulate matter* suspended in the air (dust) is extremely dangerous if the quantities are large and the exposure is frequent. *Work* is also a physical stressor.

In order to evaluate your exposure to the following stressors in your environment, please complete the following form.

SCALE 3–ENVIRONMENTAL PHYSICAL STRESSORS

Please write in the number that corresponds to your exposure to the following physical stressors in your environment. Comment or give examples to clarify your answers. Write in "X" if you do not know.

5	4	3	2	1	X
Daily	**Weekly**	**Monthly**	**Rarely**	**Never**	**Do Not Know**

1. Temperature extremes—high or low (arctic, snow skiing, desert conditions, boiler room, living in climate characterized by extreme temperature changes)   _____

Comment:_____

_____

2. Humidity extremes—high or low (hot summer days, cold winter days, desert)   _____

Comment:_____

_____

3. Barometric pressure extremes—high or low (high altitudes, airplanes, scuba diving)   _____

Comment:_____

_____

4. X-rays—above natural exposure (industrial and medical, by occupation)   _____

Comment:_____

_____

5. Trauma—direct violence exceeding normal exposure (police work, fireman, stunt man, military)   _____

Comment:_____

_____

6. Immersion—exceeding normal exposure risk (fisherman, live on water)   _____

Comment:_____

_____

7. Ultraviolet radiation—excessive (lifeguard, fisherman, farmer)   _____

Comment:_____

_____

continued

5	4	3	2	1	X
Daily	**Weekly**	**Monthly**	**Rarely**	**Never**	**Do Not Know**

8. Motion—exceeding normal (pilot, astronaut) _____

Comment:_____

_____

9. High-intensity sound (factory workers, musicians, construction workers) _____

Comment:_____

_____

10. Excessive dust (grain workers, miners, woodworkers) _____

Comment:_____

_____

11. Microwaves _____

Comment:_____

_____

12. Radio waves _____

Comment:_____

_____

13. Work (physical exertion) _____

Comment:_____

_____

14. Other: Please list and indicate frequency of exposure to other environmental _____
physical stressors of which you are aware.

_____

_____

_____ _____

_____

_____ _____

_____

_____

_____

continued

5	4	3	2	1	X
Daily	**Weekly**	**Monthly**	**Rarely**	**Never**	**Do Not Know**
					_____
					_____
15. Unknown*					_____?????_
				Total	_____

There are probably many as yet undiscovered environmental physical stressors.

The higher your score, the more intense is your exposure to physical stressors. Do not panic; exposure does not necessarily result in immediate and/or irreversible damage. The next section explains how these factors can be dealt with most effectively.

Physical Supporters

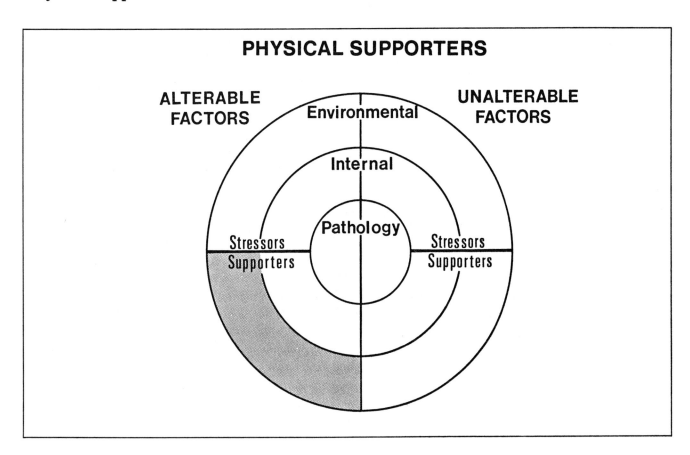

PHYSICAL SUPPORTERS
Climate Control
Heating
Ventilation
Housing
Cooling
Protective Clothing
Pressure suits
Wet suits
Fire resistant
Heat resistant
Climate control
Protective Devices
Masks
Filters
Shields
Seat belts
Air bags
Scuba equipment
Ear plugs
Pressure chambers
Sunscreens
Others

Physical Supporters: *Environmental conditions, agents, or events that tend to protect an individual from physical stressors.*

Shelter, heating, air conditioning, humidification, and ventilation are familiar to all of us, although probably taken for granted. Under conditions of potential extreme physical exposure, some less well-known supporters may be available. Special clothing is available for those who must maintain acceptable temperatures for survival in environmental conditions of heat or cold that could be lethal. Extreme environmental pressures can be compensated for by use of special clothing or pressurized chambers or vehicles. Shielded clothing and specially designed rooms and barriers can protect individuals from radiation exposure. Ultraviolet light can be blocked with simple sunscreens. Trauma can be reduced with seat belts, air bags, protective clothing, and other means. Immersion can be protected against through use of protective clothing. Dust can be avoided and can be filtered by use of masks and ventilation systems. Microwaves must be avoided through use of safe microwave ovens; and although other sources of microwaves are more difficult to control, methods are being developed to reduce exposure in industry and the general environment.

Those who are unable to avoid exposure to extremes of physical stressors because of climate or employment must employ protective devices, such as clothing, filters, shields, ear protectors, and pressure suits. Some are able to measure the exposure they receive over a given period of time and keep within "safe" limits. X-ray exposure can be measured on a cumulative-dose basis, and "safe" limits for exposure have been set.*

If you are unaware of any personal exposure to the extremes of physical stressors, that does not mean that you are unexposed. You should learn what you are being exposed to on a daily basis. In addition, physical stressors within the normal limits of exposure are potentially dangerous under certain circumstances. For example, temperature extremes have a definite effect on exercise tolerance. Extremes in humidity and high and low temperatures within the normal range of our climate reduce exercise tolerance. These may be dangerous factors even for a healthy, conditioned individual, but their effect may well be fatal for the person with a major medical problem such as heart disease. Changes of barometric pressure within the range of normal have a major effect on the way most people function. Many people report specific ailments with increased frequency during changes of barometric pressure associated with weather fronts moving in. This is particularly true of arthritis patients.

The fact is that we are unable to avoid exposure to all physical stressors. For this reason, they must be acknowledged where appropriate, and we must take steps to reduce their effects on us. More and more information becomes available on the subject of physical stressors daily. Your doctor will probably be able to provide you with additional information regarding this topic if you ask.†

*Safe limits are set by regulatory agencies and remain controversial.
†Many publications are available from the Superintendent of Documents, U.S. Government Printing Office, Washington, D.C. 20402.

Chemical Stressors

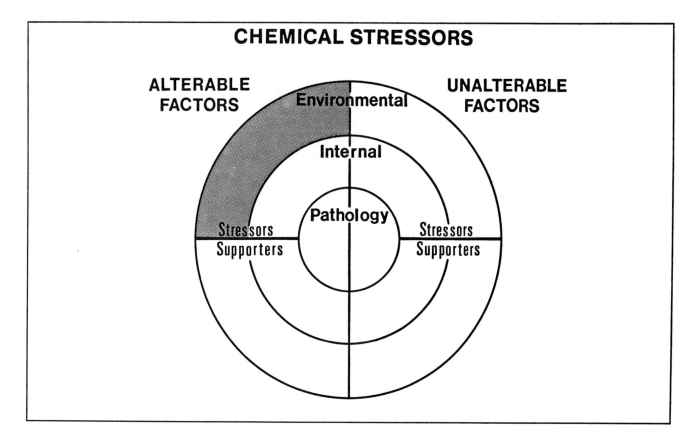

Chemical Stressors: *Environmental chemical agents to which you are potentially or actually exposed and that are known to have an adverse effect on man.*

Many of these factors are experienced by many of us on a daily basis. *Carbon monoxide* is a gas by-product of the incomplete combustion of hydrocarbons, such as gasoline used as fuel in automobiles and other vehicles and power tools. *Sodium chloride* is table salt. In addition to that which we add to our food, the salt used on our roads has a tendency to seep into water supplies. *Prescription* and *nonprescription drugs* are relied on by many of us on an alarmingly frequent basis. What we have a tendency to ignore is the fact that there are potential major side effects to virtually every drug. *Insecticides* are a normal part of the commercial production of fruits and vegetables. Not only are they applied externally, but some are also used systemically to prevent insect infestations; thus they are a part of the food and cannot be washed off! And, they enter the environment and may enter the food chain and be ingested when eating wild fish, fowl, game, and livestock. Cow's milk may contain insecticides and other concentrated toxins.

Preservatives are found in virtually every food type on the market. Their effects on the body are unknown, but there are many suspicions regarding some of them. The health effects of *food additives,* such as

CHEMICAL STRESSORS	
Carbon monoxide	Hydrocarbons
Sodium chloride	Nitrogen dioxide
Prescription drugs	Mercury
Nonprescription drugs	Asbestos
	Nicotine
Insecticides	Tar
Preservatives	Hormones in consumer products
Food additives	
Chlorine compounds	Antibiotics in consumer products
Fluoride	
Lead salts	Alcohol
Ammonia	Monosodium glutamate
Chlorine gas	
Xanthines	Spices
Ozone	Other exhaust gases
Hydrogen sulfide	Others known and unknown

artificial color, artificial flavor, flavor enhancers, and texturizers are also unknown for the most part. However, many are suspect, and some are known to produce certain illnesses. *Monosodium glutamate* (MSG) is a very commonly used flavor enhancer. It is known to produce the "Chinese restaurant syndrome," which is a conglomeration of symptoms that result from consumption of sufficient amounts of MSG. *Spices* are thought by some researchers to be more of a problem than mere producers of indigestion. Some have been linked to hyperactivity and other medical problems. *Nitrites* and *nitrates* are converted to nitrosamines in cooking. Nitrosamines are also found in many beers. They are known to be carcinogens. *Chlorine* is added to many water supplies to destroy bacteria, but chlorine in combination with other water contaminants appears to be a carcinogen. *Fluoride* is also added to many water supplies because its beneficial effects against tooth decay are known and have been measured. However, its use is still controversial, and some consider its use in water supplies to be dangerous.

Lead salts are extremely toxic, as are all heavy metal salts, and lead is a very common environmental contaminant. It is toxic when either inhaled or ingested. Lead is found in the atmosphere as a result of the combustion of leaded gasoline and of lead itself in, for example, automobile batteries at dumps. It is also found in colored newspaper and magazine print and can enter the atmosphere when these are burned. Children who chew on newspapers and other printed materials can develop lead poisoning. Some older homes or apartments have paint that contains lead that can be ingested and/or enter the air through burning. Other potential sources of lead poisoning include handling of molten lead and drinking water from systems with old lead pipes which have not been replaced with copper. *Mercury* poisoning has resulted from industrial pollution of water followed by concentration in the fish food chain with resultant high concentrations in fish eaten by man. *Copper* poisoning can result from the leaching of copper from pipes by acid water.

Ammonia, as in household ammonia, is a potential toxin. Noxious gases can be released through combination of chlorine bleach with common ammonia cleaners or old urine-soaked cloth. *Xanthines* are potentially toxic stimulants; caffeine is found in coffee, theophylline in tea, and theobromine in chocolate. Some herbal teas are also toxic. *Ozone* is a toxic gas that results from the use of electric motors or from electrical storms. The gas *hydrogen sulfide* is given off in the process of paper production and other processes involving the use of wood and wood pulp. This gas produces a strong odor in small concentrations and is toxic or poisonous in high concentrations when inhaled. *Hydrocarbons* are organic compounds of hydrogen and carbon; most are toxic and are the result of the distillation of petroleum. They are toxic primarily by ingestion (swallowing) but can also be toxic by inhalation and can have a toxic effect on the skin. Hydrocarbons are also inhaled in the smoke of cigarettes, and the burning of plastics is associated with some particularly noxious gases. *Waste oil* and *solvents* have been found in drinking water and have been known to contaminate even deep wells. Their source is usually refinery or industrial waste, waste oil dumping sites, and common household cleaners. Some are also known to be carcinogenic as well as toxic. *Nitrogen dioxide* is found in automobile exhaust and other exhaust gases that result from combustion and other sources. There are many other toxic gases in the exhaust of incinerators and smokestacks, both industrial and private.

Asbestos, a mineral known to be carcinogenic and to produce several lung diseases, is a problem when inhaled. Exposure is primarily industrial or it may be accidental in buildings with asbestos components. *Nicotine,* a potent insecticide, is a stimulant of the cardiovascular and nervous system. It is found in the tobacco leaf and in the smoke inhaled by the tobacco smoker or in the juice of chewed tobacco. Tars from tobacco smoke are well known carcinogens.

Hormones are chemicals that are naturally produced in animals. However, in addition to their use as drugs by physicians, they are added to the feed of commercially grown animals such as cows and chickens to increase the speed of weight gain in the animal. However, there are residual quantities in the meat consumed in the home. Although "safe" levels are required before the meat can go to market, we do not know the effect of these residual concentrations. *Antibiotics* are also added to certain animal feeds for the suppression of infections. Residual concentrations, again, are found in the meat that is marketed, and some researchers have postulated that allergic problems and resistant strains of bacteria result from its consumption. *Alcohol* is a commonly consumed toxic chemical. Consumption in excess of one ounce of alcohol per day is known to be destructive to the body. In addition, there are other hydrocarbons in many of the distilled spirits. Many of them are known to be toxic. Tranquilizers and sleeping pills are commonly used both legally and illegally. They are frequently prescribed by physicians. Their use should be avoided. If prescribed by your doctor, ask if it is absolutely necessary that they be used.

The following scale includes most of the known major chemical stressors but is certainly not complete. The state of knowledge concerning this material is constantly changing. New chemicals are being introduced at a very rapid rate. If you are being exposed to chemicals that are not listed, please add them to the end of the scale and indicate your exposure.

SCALE 4–ENVIRONMENTAL CHEMICAL STRESSORS

Please fill out the following checklist in order to measure your exposure to the following chemical stressors.

Write in the number that corresponds to your experience.

I am or have been exposed to the following chemicals:

5	4	3	2	1	X
Daily	**Weekly**	**Monthly**	**Rarely**	**Never**	**Do Not Know**

PAST TWO WEEKS	PAST YEAR				
_____	_____	**1.** Carbon monoxide (exhaust gas) Comment: _____			
_____	_____	**2.** Sodium chloride, i.e., table salt (or some contaminated drinking water) Comment: _____			

continued

5	4	3	2	1	X
Daily	**Weekly**	**Monthly**	**Rarely**	**Never**	**Do Not Know**
PAST TWO WEEKS	PAST YEAR				

_____   _____   **3.** Prescription drugs

Comment: _____

_____

_____   _____   **4.** Nonprescription drugs

Comment: _____

_____

_____   _____   **5.** Insecticides and herbicides

Comment: _____

_____

_____   _____   **6.** Preservatives

Comment: _____

_____

_____   _____   **7.** Food additives such as artificial color, artificial flavor, flavor enhancers, texturizers

Comment: _____

_____

_____   _____   **8.** Chlorine (drinking water)

Comment: _____

_____

_____   _____   **9.** Fluoride (drinking water, vitamins)

Comment: _____

_____

_____   _____   **10.** Lead salts (lead glazes on pottery, gasoline exhaust, burning or melting lead)

Comment: _____

_____

_____   _____   **11.** Ammonia (household ammonia)

Comment: _____

_____

_____   _____   **12.** Chloramines (mixture of ammonia and chlorine bleach or chlorine bleach and urine-soaked clothing)

Comment: _____

_____

_____   _____   **13.** Xanthines (coffee, tea, chocolate, cola drinks)

Comment: _____

_____

continued

5	4	3	2	1	X
Daily	**Weekly**	**Monthly**	**Rarely**	**Never**	**Do Not Know**
PAST TWO WEEKS	PAST YEAR				

14. Ozone (electric motors, electrical contacts, electrical storms, welding, high humidity, pollution, summer days)

Comment: _____

15. Hydrogen sulfide (pulp mills and other wood-product factories)

Comment: _____

16. Hydrocarbons (refineries, waste oil, home use, industrial use)

Comment: _____

17. Other toxic gases (dumps, incinerators and other smokestacks, both industrial and private, and cigarette consumption)

Comment: _____

18. Nitrogen oxides (automobile exhaust and other exhaust)

Comment: _____

19. Mercury (industrial waste via food chain, for example, contaminated fish)

Comment: _____

20. Asbestos (industrial and accidental exposure in buildings with asbestos components)

Comment: _____

21. Nicotine (tobacco smoke, juice, and insecticides)

Comment: _____

22. Tar (tobacco smoke)

Comment: _____

23. Hormones in consumer products (beef and chicken)

Comment: _____

continued

5	4	3	2	1	X
Daily	**Weekly**	**Monthly**	**Rarely**	**Never**	**Do Not Know**
PAST TWO WEEKS	PAST YEAR				

_____	_____	**24.** Antibiotics in consumer products (pork and chicken)
		Comment: _____
		_____
_____	_____	**25.** Alcohol
		Comment: _____
		_____
_____	_____	**26.** Monosodium glutamate (MSG)
		Comment: _____
		_____
_____	_____	**27.** Spices
		Comment: _____
		_____
_____	_____	**28.** Others (please list and give frequency of exposure)
		Comment: _____
		_____
_____	_____	_____
_____	_____	_____
?????	?????	**29.** Unmeasurable and unknowns*
		Comment: _____
		_____
		_____
		_____

Please answer "Yes" or "No" to the following question.

_____	_____	**30.** My drinking water has been checked and is chemically pure.
No (2)	Yes (1)	
_____	_____	
Totals		

*There are probably many as yet undiscovered chemical stressors. Tune into your news media for the latest bulletins!

The higher your score, the greater your exposure to the chemical stressors in your environment. The lower your score, the lower your exposure to such stressors. Count up the number of your "X" responses. There should be a very few. If you have more than two or three, then you need to become more aware of your pattern of exposure. Chemical stressors should be avoided. In fact, there is no substitute for their avoidance, since doing so reduces the chances of diseases with which they are associated.

How Concerned Should You Be About Being Exposed to Chemicals in the Environment?

While heavy exposure to most of the listed chemicals can result in serious damage and even death, usual exposure does not necessarily result in immediate major irreversible damage. Your exposure to most of the chemicals is likely to be fairly frequent but at low levels. You may, however, be able to reduce your level of exposure even more. You are encouraged to do so. (Some of you, by virtue of occupation and/or choice of recreation, may be exposed to relatively high levels of certain chemicals at a relatively high frequency. The hazards obviously are increased for you.)

All exposure can be reduced through minimal effort. Food additives can be avoided by all of us by merely reading the labels on the packages of the food we are buying and avoiding foods with additives. Avoid the antibiotics and hormones generally fed commercial livestock and poultry by reducing your consumption of commercially grown meat and/or by carefully eliminating the fats from these meats. Wash fruits and vegetables in order to minimize your consumption of insecticides from commercially grown foods.

Your drinking water can be tested for chemical purity, and this should be done at least once. If you are drinking town or city water, check to find out what the detailed chemical analysis of the water shows. Ask about contaminants. Insist that your local government provide you with a report and review it with your doctor. If chlorine is added to your water, you will have to decide whether or not you want to consume it. Avoidance of coffee, tea, and chocolate is your choice. In small quantities, they have no known ill effects. You should keep your consumption to a minimum in order to avoid toxic effects of these stimulants. Any amount in excess of one to two cups of regular coffee or tea daily is likely to produce toxic effects. If you have experienced their ill effects, you will know how to judge your limits. (It should be noted that the signs and symptoms of caffeine poisoning mimic many of the signs and symptoms of psychosocial stress. See Chapter 2, page 9.)

Check your household for chemicals. Assume that they are all poisons either by inhalation, consumption, or contact. Make sure that they are used with care and kept out of children's reach. Beware of the use of chlorine bleach on urine-soaked clothing.

Avoid drugs of all kinds. If your doctor prescribes a drug for you, review its use with him. If it is not absolutely necessary, tell him you would prefer not to use it.

The following section will give additional directions as to how you can deal with your exposure.

Chemical Supporters

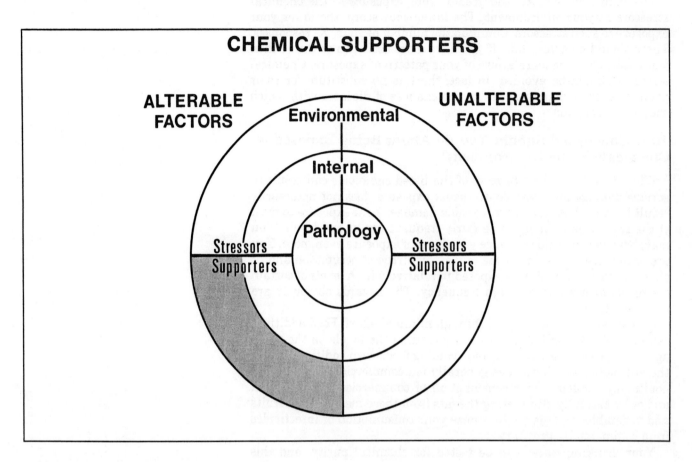

CHEMICAL SUPPORTERS
Food
Water
Vitamins A, B, C, and E
Drugs
Others

Chemical Supporters: *Environmental chemical agents to which you are potentially or actually exposed and that tend to counteract adverse effects of chemical stressors.*

Certain chemicals, chemical supporters, are known to partially counteract some adverse chemical effects. Ascorbic acid (vitamin C) is considered to be a detoxifier, that is, a chemical that tends to help eliminate toxins from the body. Vitamin E is also thought to have a role as a detoxifier. Vitamin A and some of the other vitamins probably play a role in protecting the body from ingested or inhaled toxins. There are certain prescription drugs that are administered under circumstances of acute intoxication with certain chemicals. Water plays a crucial role in the elimination of toxins from the body by virtue of its being a vehicle for excretion of body wastes in the urine. Consumption of large volumes (approximately two quarts) of high quality water (free of contaminants) may be one of the best means of protection from chemical stressors. Indeed, food in general is a conglomeration of chemicals: vitamins, minerals, carbohydrates, fats, and proteins essential to life and health. Food is the essence of a natural chemical supporter. It allows for growth, detoxification, healing, and maintenance of normal bodily function. (See Diet and Nutrition, Chap. 4.)

If you or some member of your family is acutely exposed to any large volume of chemicals or is experiencing symptoms as a result of exposure to chemicals, you should immediately check with a doctor to determine the possible need for treatment. If your exposure involves small doses of chemicals over a long period of time, you may never experience any obvious symptoms. No matter what type of exposure you are experiencing, you should strive to minimize it. If you are unable to eliminate exposure because of conditions of employment or other reasons, then you must be sure that you are using adequate safeguards to reduce the effect of exposure. The issue of exposure to chemicals at work must be taken up with the employer and your personal physician or someone whom he recommends.

The fact is that you cannot completely avoid or compensate for chemical stressors. However, knowledge of their potential hazards and an awareness of your personal exposure to them is essential to your exercising the control over your health that you do have. You can take the necessary steps to protect yourself and your family.

Biological Stressors

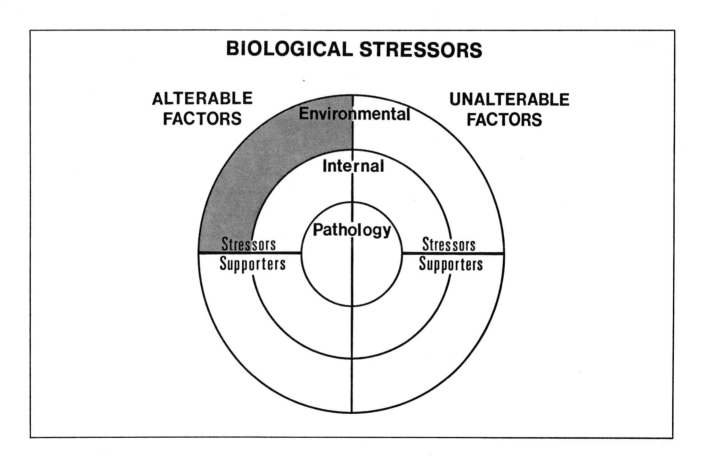

Biological Stressors: *Organisms in the environment to which you are exposed and that are known to have potentially adverse effects on man.*

Bacteria, of which there are hundreds of varieties, cause a majority of the serious infections in this country. Your exposure to them is either direct or indirect. Direct exposure results from person-to-person spread; indirect exposure takes place through food, water, insect carriers (vectors), or other intermediate hosts and objects. The *viruses*

BIOLOGICAL STRESSORS
Bacteria
Viruses
Rickettsiae
Chlamydiae
Fungi
Protozoa (single-celled animals)
Metazoa (multicellular animals)
Plants (single and multicellular)
Other

that can infect man are even more numerous and varied than the bacteria. However, as a rule, viral infections are less severe than bacterial infections. Some, however, are serious but rarely fatal. *Rickettsiae* and *Chlamydiae* are organisms which function on a level between bacteria and viruses. They are known to be infectious to man in limited numbers. However, the illnesses they cause are, as a rule, more serious than either viral or bacterial illnesses. *Fungi* usually cause relatively common skin infections. These are usually annoying but minor. There are, however, more serious localized and generalized infections that can result from fungi. *Protozoa,* or single-celled animals, cause a limited amount of disease in developed countries. They are the agents of malaria, amebiasis, giardiasis, trichomoniasis, plus a few other parasitic diseases. They are, however, currently being recognized more frequently than in the past. *Metazoa,* or multicellular animals, are the cause of a majority of the world's infections. These are the predominant *parasites* of the world and include flatworms, roundworms, and arthropods such as scabies, lice, and mites. Fleas, chiggers, mosquitoes, ticks, sand flies, flies, and other pests are carriers (vectors) of disease. *Venomous insects* such as ants, caterpillars, wasps, bees, hornets, spiders, and scorpions usually cause temporary pain. However, a venomous sting to an allergic individual may be life-threatening if not fatal. Certain *fish* are known to be poisonous if consumed and venomous if touched. Certain *snakes* are well known to all of us as being poisonous. This is also true of *rare lizards* and *toads.* Rare *exotic snails* are venomous, as are certain types of *coral* and other *marine animals,* such as the sea anemone and jellyfish. Larger members of the animal kingdom are rarely directly hazardous to the health of man. However, for those of us who venture off into the wilderness, there is the remote danger of an animal attack.

Many *plants* are poisonous when eaten and many cause rashes when touched. This even includes certain house and garden plants such as daffodils, castor bean, foxglove, iris, rhubarb (the leaf), and many others.

In order to evaluate your exposure to biological stressors, please fill out the following questionnaire.

SCALE 5–ENVIRONMENTAL BIOLOGICAL STRESSORS

Please indicate the frequency with which you follow the listed behavior.

5	4	3	2	1	X
Never	**Rarely**	**Sometimes**	**Usually**	**Always**	**Do Not Know**

_____ **1.** I wash my hands before eating.

Comment: _____

_____

_____ **2.** I keep my hands out of my mouth.

Comment: _____

_____

continued

5	4	3	2	1	X
Never	Rarely	Sometimes	Usually	Always	Do Not Know

_____ **3.** I avoid sick people.

Comment: _____

_____

_____ **4.** I avoid drinking out of someone else's glass.

Comment: _____

_____

_____ **5.** I have checked my water supply and know that it is pure (free from harmful bacteria).

Comment: _____

_____

_____ **6.** I make sure my immunizations are up to date.

Comment: _____

_____

_____ **7.** When I travel to foreign countries, I follow recommended immunization practice and malaria prevention.

Comment: _____

_____

_____ **8.** I limit my sexual experience to my spouse or preferred sexual partner. (This reduces exposure to venereal diseases.)

Comment: _____

_____

_____ **9.** I avoid venomous and poisonous animals.

Comment: _____

_____

_____ **10.** I refrigerate food immediately after meals. (This reduces exposure to bacteria and reduces chances of food poisoning.)

Comment: _____

_____

_____ **11.** I remove the stuffing from the turkey immediately after cooking. (This reduces exposure to salmonella, a type of bacterium that causes food poisoning.)

Comment: _____

_____

_____ **12.** I boil my water when out on camping trips. (Reduces exposure to bacteria that can cause poisoning.)

Comment: _____

_____

_____

continued

5	4	3	2	1	X
Never	**Rarely**	**Sometimes**	**Usually**	**Always**	**Do Not Know**

_____ **13.** I boil canned vegetables before eating them. (Reduces risk of botulism and other problems with bacteria.)

Comment: _____

_____

_____ **14.** When doing my home canning, I follow the directions from a reputable book and the manufacturer of the canning material. (Reduces chances of food poisoning.)

Comment: _____

_____

_____ **15.** I don't kiss pets or let them eat off my dishes. (Reduces chances of exposure to worms and pet infections.)

Comment: _____

_____

_____ **16.** I avoid sick animals and birds, domestic or wild. (Reduces chances of exposure to pet infections.)*

Comment: _____

_____

_____ **17.** I wear shoes when walking in sandy soil. (Avoids hookworms.)

Comment: _____

_____

_____ **18.** I avoid eating seafood that is known to be toxic. (Certain fish and shellfish are toxic at certain times of the year, e.g., clams during red tide.)

Comment: _____

_____

_____ **19.** I avoid eating wild mushrooms.

Comment: _____

_____

_____ **20.** I do not eat wild plants, berries, and nuts unless I am sure they are edible.

Comment: _____

_____

_____ **21.** After walking in the country, I wash carefully. (Reduces risk of contact rashes, e.g., poison ivy.)

Comment: _____

_____

_____ **22.** Other_____

_____ _____

_____ _____

_____ _____

_____ _____

continued

5	4	3	2	1	X
Never	**Rarely**	**Sometimes**	**Usually**	**Always**	**Do Not Know**

_____??????_____   **23.** Unmeasurable and unknown.

Comment: _____

_____

_____

Total

Pregnant women should avoid kittens and kitty litter to reduce chances of toxoplasmosis.

The higher your score, the more likely you are to be exposed or susceptible to biological stressors. Exposure does not necessarily result in infection. If your exposure is minimal, you are less likely to have a serious problem. The larger the "dose" of infecting organism, the more likely you are to become infected. However, the condition of the host at the time of exposure is also very important. A weak or malnourished individual is more likely to become infected than a healthy, well-nourished individual. Proper diet is very important in maintaining high resistance to infection and in promoting rapid healing once infected. In addition, it appears that a well-nourished individual in good condition has fewer symptoms than the poorly nourished and/or unconditioned one. Immunization improves resistance to infection (see Immunity, page 115). If you have any "X" responses, investigate further and find out the answers. You may be subjected to other stressors you did not know about that you can influence favorably.

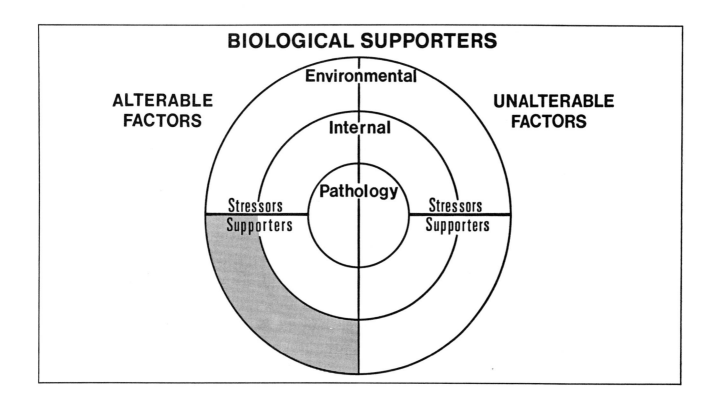

BIOLOGICAL SUPPORTERS
Nutrient Source—Food
Single-celled animals
Multicellular animals
Single-celled plants
Multicellular plants

Biological Supporters: *Organisms in the environment that tend to have a healing effect on man.*

Although some plants and animals contribute to the hazards of the biological environment, many more are essential to man's life and health. In addition to being a major source of food for us, plants provide oxygen. Bacteria in the intestines provide vitamin K, and bacteria on the skin and in the intestines protect us from attempted invasion by other microorganisms. Microorganisms are the basis of the food chain which eventually leads to man. Viruses established within the body give off interferon, which prohibits invasion by other viruses. They may also have some other beneficial effects that are as yet unknown to us (see Diet and Nutrition, page 129).

Social Stressors

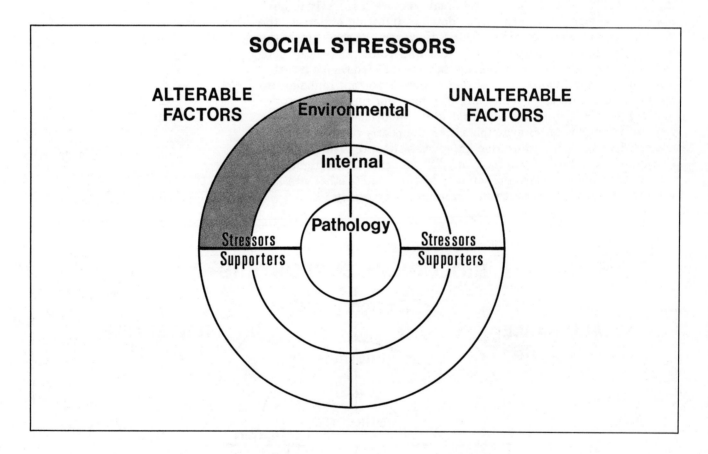

Social Stressors: *Those organizations and people to whom you relate and that are potentially stressful.*

These are the factors with which most of us are familiar. However, although we may be familiar with these factors, we are often not aware of how much stress they are producing in our lives.

SOCIAL STRESSORS	
Marriage	Recreational organizations
Family	School
Work	Friends
Church (religion)	Physician and/or other health professional
Government	Financial organizations
Neighborhood	The economy
Social organizations	
Political organizations	

In order to assess your perceived exposure to these social stressors, please fill out the following questionnaire.

SCALE 6–ENVIRONMENTAL SOCIAL STRESSORS

The following is a list of broad categories of social stressors. Please write in the number that corresponds to your experience using the following scale.

Indicate how your personal experience with the following social factors has *adversely* affected you.

5	4	3	2	1	X
Major Adverse Effect	Serious Adverse Effect	Moderate Adverse Effect	Slight Adverse Effect	Insignificant Adverse Effect	Do Not Know

PAST TWO WEEKS	PAST STRESSFUL TIMES	
_____	_____	**1.** Marriage Comment: _____
_____	_____	**2.** Family Comment: _____
_____	_____	**3.** Work Comment: _____
_____	_____	**4.** Church (religion) Comment: _____

continued

5	4	3	2	1	X
Major Adverse Effect	**Serious Adverse Effect**	**Moderate Adverse Effect**	**Slight Adverse Effect**	**Insignificant Adverse Effect**	**Do Not Know**
PAST TWO WEEKS	PAST STRESSFUL TIMES				

_____ _____ **5.** Government

Comment: _____

_____

_____ _____ **6.** Neighborhood

Comment: _____

_____

_____ _____ **7.** Social organizations

Comment: _____

_____

_____ _____ **8.** Political organizations

Comment: _____

_____

_____ _____ **9.** Recreational organizations

Comment: _____

_____

_____ _____ **10.** School

Comment: _____

_____

_____ _____ **11.** Friends

Comment: _____

_____

_____ _____ **12.** Physician and/or other health professional

Comment: _____

_____

_____ _____ **13.** Financial organizations (e.g., banks, credit unions)

Comment: _____

_____

_____ _____ **14.** The economy

Comment: _____

_____

continued

5	4	3	2	1	X
Major Adverse Effect	**Serious Adverse Effect**	**Moderate Adverse Effect**	**Slight Adverse Effect**	**Insignificant Adverse Effect**	**Do Not Know**
PAST TWO WEEKS	PAST STRESSFUL TIMES				

15. Other (please list)

_____ _____

_____ _____   _____

_____ _____   _____

_____ _____   _____

_____ _____
         Totals

The higher your scores, the more likely you are to be experiencing or to have experienced problems as a result of social stressors. Please take note of the problem areas that you have identified. Later in the book, material will be presented that will help you to examine your problems in greater detail. Take note of your "X" responses or unknown areas that you have identified. Later material will help you to examine them more closely and determine whether or not you do have problems in those areas.

Environmental Social Supporters

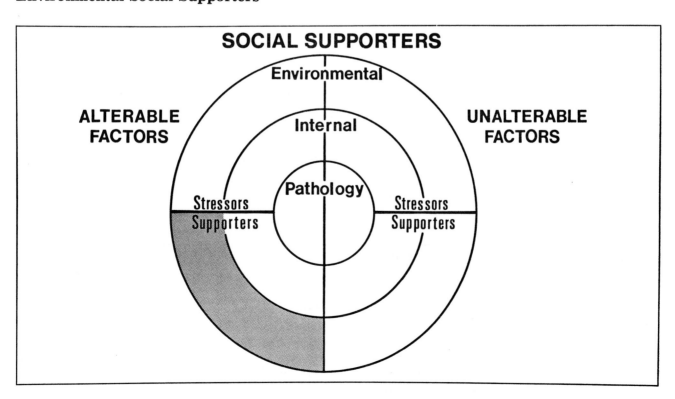

Social Supporters: *Those organizations and people to whom you relate and that tend to have a healing effect and that protect you from social stressors.*

SOCIAL SUPPORTERS

Marriage	Recreational organizations
Family	School
Work	Friends
Church (religion)	Physician and/or other health professional
Government	
Neighborhood	Financial organizations
Social organizations	The economy
Political organizations	

In order to assess your perception of the social supporters that you do have, please fill out the following questionnaire. Again, these are broad categories. Please write in the number corresponding to your experience using the following scale.

SCALE 7–ENVIRONMENTAL SOCIAL SUPPORTERS

Please indicate how the following social supporters affect your life. Indicate how your personal experience with the following social factors has benefited you.

5	4	3	2	1	X
No Healing Effect	Slight Healing Effect	Moderate Healing Effect	Great Healing Effect	Major Healing Effect	Unknown

PAST TWO WEEKS	PAST STRESSFUL TIMES				
_____	_____	**1.** Marriage			
		Comment: _____			
_____	_____	**2.** Family			
		Comment: _____			
_____	_____	**3.** Work			
		Comment: _____			
_____	_____	**4.** Church			
		Comment: _____			
_____	_____	**5.** Government			
		Comment: _____			

5	4	3	2	1	X
No Healing Effect	Slight Healing Effect	Moderate Healing Effect	Great Healing Effect	Major Healing Effect	Unknown
PAST TWO WEEKS	PAST STRESSFUL TIMES				

————— ————— **6.** Neighborhood

Comment: ————————————————————

————————————————————————————

————— ————— **7.** Social organizations

Comment: ————————————————————

————————————————————————————

————— ————— **8.** Political organizations

Comment: ————————————————————

————————————————————————————

————— ————— **9.** Recreational organizations

Comment: ————————————————————

————————————————————————————

————— ————— **10.** School

Comment: ————————————————————

————————————————————————————

————— ————— **11.** Friends

Comment: ————————————————————

————————————————————————————

————— ————— **12.** Physician and/or other health professional

Comment: ————————————————————

————————————————————————————

————— ————— **13.** Financial organizations (e.g., banks, credit unions)

Comment: ————————————————————

————————————————————————————

————— ————— **14.** The economy

Comment: ————————————————————

————————————————————————————

————— ————— **15.** Other (please list)

————————————————————————————

————— ————— ————————————————————————————

————— ————— ————————————————————————————

————— ————— ————————————————————————————

————— ————— ————————————————————————————

————— —————   Totals

The higher your scores, the less likely you are to be getting the help you need from those around you. Please take notice of the categories with the highest scores. You will have the opportunity to explore these areas in greater detail and see how you may be able to improve your situation for the future. In addition, note your "X" responses. Remember the areas when these issues are brought up later in the book in the section devoted to Interpersonal Style and your Support Network (pages 63–69).

INTERNAL FACTORS

We will now begin to examine some of the internal factors, or factors within the individual, that have a significant effect on health and well-being. The general categories, as you will recall from examining the Integrated Model, include individual attitude, behavior, genetic makeup, and immunity. Pregnancy, lactation (breastfeeding), and menstruation are special nonpathological internal conditions that have major effects on the individual adult even in the absence of disease or pathology. (See Special Conditions, page 119.) In addition, the absence or presence of pathology or disease and its seriousness play a major role in stress tolerance. Let us now examine these factors in more detail.

Attitudinal Stressors

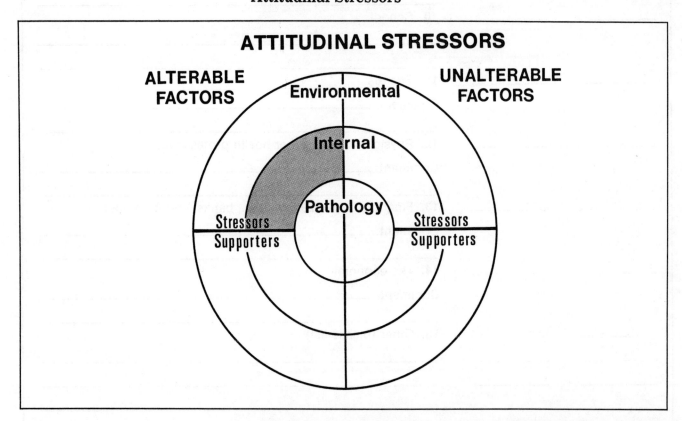

ATTITUDINAL STRESSORS

ALTERABLE FACTORS

UNALTERABLE FACTORS

Environmental

Internal

Pathology

Stressors
Supporters

Stressors
Supporters

Attitudinal Stressors: *Those attitudes and beliefs about one's self and others that lead to inaccurate perception and unhealthy interpretations of self, others, and events.*

ATTITUDINAL STRESSORS

Negative self-image

Excessive self-criticism

Excessively high need for approval

Excessively high need for achievement

Unrealistically high need for control of others or events

Perceived loss of control or influence over others or events

Unreasonable expectations of others

Unreasonable expectations of self

Lack of awareness of personal responsibility

Inability to acknowledge and accept one's emotions

Inappropriate willingness to change

Attitudinal Supporters

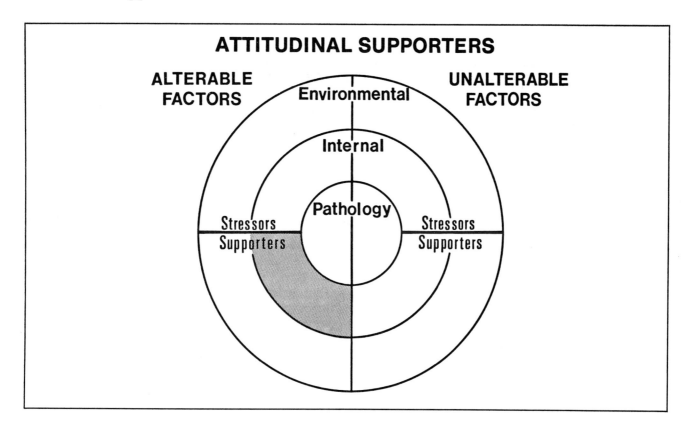

Attitudinal Supporters: *Those attitudes and beliefs about one's self and others that promote accurate perceptions and healthy interpretations of self, others, and events.*

Interaction of Attitudinal Stressors and Supporters

A large component of the stress which we experience is due to emotional factors. Ten people would probably experience ten different intensity levels of stress in the same situation. Why? The experience of stress has more to do with how we interpret the meaning of a situation

ATTITUDINAL SUPPORTERS

Accurate self-image

Acceptance of personal limitations

Recognition of personal strengths

Liking oneself

Reasonable, achievable goals for self and others

Realistic assessment of one's ability to control and influence others and events

Acceptance of responsibility for one's behavior and emotions

Appropriate willingness to change

and/or our role in a situation than it does with the direct impact of the environment on our bodies. For example, an ambiguous job evaluation could mean imminent dismissal to the insecure employee or it could mean "I'm doing well enough" to the secure employee. A spouse saying "I'm tired" to a sexual overture may mean "I'm tired" to the secure spouse and "I don't want you" to the insecure lover. There is usually enough ambiguity in any situation or communication so that we can elect to pay attention to what we expect to find.

The major cause of stress problems comes from the pressure we put on ourselves. People who are prone to stress-related physical and emotional reactions tend to have unrealistically high personal goals either in terms of achievement or approval from others. They tend to view themselves as personally responsible for events and persons beyond their actual control. They often have low self-esteem or tie their self-appraisal to recognition from others. Recognizing how you create stress for yourself is half the battle. Learning, then, to minimize the harmful effects of self-induced stress can mitigate the worst effects of these characteristics.

SCALE 8–ATTITUDINAL STRESSORS AND SUPPORTERS

Look over the following checklist and mark those that seem to apply to you.* This will provide you with material to begin understanding the relationship between your perceptions of reality and your stress.

Rate each question from 5 to 1 depending on how much you seem to exhibit these characteristics.

5	4	3	2	1
Just Like Me	**Very Much Like Me**	**Somewhat Like Me**	**A Little Like Me**	**Not at All Like Me**

_____   **1.** What people think about me personally and/or professionally is very important. If I think someone doesn't have high regard for me and/or my work, I think about that a lot and am bothered by it.

Comment: _____

_____

_____   **2.** I don't like people to be angry with me. I want to be liked by as many people as possible.

Comment: _____

_____

_____   **3.** For fear of angering others, I will often avoid saying or doing things that I believe ought to be said or done. I probably should be more assertive, but worry about hurting others' feelings or the risk that they'll get angry with me.

Comment: _____

_____

*See footnote p. 44.   *continued*

5	4	3	2	1
Just Like Me	Very Much Like Me	Somewhat Like Me	A Little Like Me	Not at All Like Me

_____ **4.** I will sometimes make important decisions that affect my life (i.e., how I spend my time, do my job, order my priorities) on the basis of what someone who is important to me wants me to do. I would rather try to please them than do something that would disappoint or upset them even if it means that I am not doing things "my way."

Comment: _____

_____

_____ **5.** Winning is important to me. I often feel competitive with others or myself. Coming in second is not acceptable. I should always strive to be the best.

Comment: _____

_____

_____ **6.** Being efficient is very important to me. I don't like wasting time. I try to get in as much as possible in the time available. I can become annoyed with interruptions or delays. I find that I usually do the work better than those around me.

Comment: _____

_____

_____ **7.** Getting ahead in life is very important. I don't like to "settle." Promotion and/or the "finer things in life" are an essential part of my feeling successful.

Comment: _____

_____

_____ **8.** I like and respect myself more when I am working effectively and getting praise and recognition. I often feel bad about myself when I don't think I am succeeding as I should. (See footnote, page 44.)

Comment: _____

_____

_____ **9.** I feel like I am responsible for seeing that things on the job go well, that people under me do their jobs without mistakes, and that errors made by my subordinates are my responsibility. When I see things going wrong, it is my responsibility to try to improve them.

Comment: _____

_____

_____ **10.** I feel that the behavior of family members is a reflection of how good a spouse and/or parent I am.

Comment: _____

_____

continued

5	4	3	2	1
Just Like Me	**Very Much Like Me**	**Somewhat Like Me**	**A Little Like Me**	**Not at All Like Me**

_____ **11.** When things do not go well, I tend to think about the worst possible outcome. I tend to worry too much about what might happen and/or about things outside my control.

Comment: _____

_____

_____ **12.** I often feel slightly guilty when not working on something. Vacation time is difficult for me if I do not have a worthwhile project to complete.

Comment: _____

_____

_____ **13.** I have trouble enjoying "free time" outside of my work or responsibilities. I do not have hobbies and projects that I find relaxing.

Comment: _____

_____

_____ **14.** My family and/or colleagues say I work too hard for my own good. My spouse and/or family complain I am not home enough or relaxed enough.

Comment: _____

_____

*The terms "work," "job," and "employment" in this workbook are used in the broadest sense. Monetary reimbursement is not the criterion for "work." Household management and/or child care is considered work. This type of contribution to a family or relationship is often overlooked if only activities that produce income are defined as work. In fact, because child care and household management are rarely defined as work, the stress of such a job with open-ended hours, no pay, and little or no recognition can exceed the stress of socially recognized employment situations. Under these circumstances, the lines between personal life and work life for the household manager are blurred or invisible. Problems stemming from the work pressure of running a home and caring for children spill over into the personal relationships, producing problems in the marriage or in parenting. Unless the multiple roles of the household manager are identified and separated from other personal roles, the origin of the stress for the household manager is often confused. On all scales in this text, those individuals who perform the role of homemaker and/or are involved in child care should consider those activities their "employment" and answer the questions from that framework.

THE NEED FOR APPROVAL: QUESTIONS 1 TO 4. Man is a social animal. We all need approval, recognition, and attention to motivate us, and to help us feel accepted and valued by others. However, when the need for approval overrides everything else, problems result. The quality of decisions often suffers because the determining factor is the opinion of others, not the merits of the issue. Stress is nearly always a by-product because the individual must be concerned at all times about how his behavior will be received. Enormous energy is spent watching for other people's reactions.

If your score for these four questions is high, your need for approval is likely to be a problem to you. An excessively high need for approval is usually associated with a background in which the individual was unsure of love and acceptance and/or where approval and love were contingent on "acceptable" behavior. Individuals with very high need for approval typically have a fairly low self-esteem and feel good about themselves only when approved of by others, all the while working hard to maintain that approval because of fear of rejection.

The solution to this painful situation is to evaluate and revise your self-image so that it is not as susceptible to the whims of others. The chart that follows will be a helpful start. However, changing your self-image can be difficult without the help of an objective second person. Professional counseling is very beneficial in these situations.

SCALE 9–SELF-IMAGE CHART

When answering the following questions use adjectives and/or very *brief,* specific descriptions to answer questions A through E.

When you have recorded your perceptions about yourself on paper, evaluate the validity of those perceptions. (We tend to carry our concept of ourselves around like baggage year after year without reevaluating its current accuracy. An inaccurate image of yourself, particularly negative perceptions, can dramatically alter your behavior and create considerable stress.) Look at what you have written about yourself under categories A through D. In the Comments column, indicate the evidence that supports your view. How do you *know* your view is accurate? *Who* told you you are this way? On what experiences from your past are you basing these conclusions? How long have you believed these things about yourself? If once true, are they still accurate?

For Category E, indicate *specifically* what you would need to do to accomplish your goals of changing in the desired directions. Then list the excuses you make to justify your not trying to change.

Self-Image Assessment Chart

ASSESSMENT AREA	COMMENTS
A. What Do I Like About Myself? **1.** On the job*	
2. Off the job	
B. What Do I Dislike About Myself? **1.** On the job	

continued

Self-Image Assessment Chart

ASSESSMENT AREA	COMMENTS

2. Off the job

_____
_____
_____
_____
_____

C. What Do I Think Other People Like About Me?
   1. On the job

_____
_____
_____
_____
_____
_____

   2. Off the job

_____
_____
_____
_____
_____

D. What Do I Think Other People Dislike About Me?
   1. On the job

_____
_____
_____
_____
_____

   2. Off the job

_____
_____
_____
_____
_____

continued

Self-Image Assessment Chart		
	WHAT DO I NEED TO DO TO ACHIEVE THESE GOALS?	WHAT EXCUSES DO I USE TO AVOID TRYING TO CHANGE?
E. How Would I Like To Be Different? **1.** On the job		
2. Off the job		

*"Job" refers also to those roles, whether taken by men or women, that include the primary responsibility for running the home and raising the family. Nonreimbursed work of this type is considered employment (see footnote, page 44).

THE NEED FOR ACHIEVEMENT: QUESTIONS 5 TO 8. Clearly, most successful people have a fairly high desire to achieve, to perfect their skills, to gain positions of influence and power, or to become recognized by their peers. This is often a strong motivating force for beneficial change in the individual and society. However, as with the need for approval, the person whose self-esteem is tied directly to recognition by others runs the risk of serious stress. To say, "I'm OK only if others believe I am doing well" places your self-image captive to the evaluation of others. Since the definition of "success" varies enormously from family to family, culture to culture, job to job, it would be impossible to keep everyone impressed all the time. Under these conditions, recognition, not the pleasure of doing a job well or reaping earned rewards, becomes the motive for behavior. Such people drive themselves toward unrealistic and often unachievable goals, accepting nothing short of perfection before they relax and enjoy satisfaction. More difficult still is the person who sets his goals far higher than he would expect from others and will not feel satisfied even when others are satisfied with him. It is useful to ask yourself the following questions periodically, especially if your score was high on the preceding series of questions.

ASSESSMENT CHART: THE NEED FOR ACHIEVEMENT

1. What are my personal goals?

Comment:_____

_____

_____

2. What are my professional work or employment goals?

Comment:_____

_____

_____

3. Are these really *my* goals or the goals of others: my parents, spouse, friends, boss?

Comment:_____

_____

_____

4. What measurement of success do I use for each of the above?

Comment:_____

_____

_____

_____

5. How and how often do I "reward" myself for my achievements?

Comment:_____

_____

_____

_____

6. Are these goals and my criteria achievable?

Comment:_____

_____

_____

_____

7. Do I expect much more of myself than I do of others? If yes, why am I a special case? Who expects this of me other than myself?

Comment:_____

_____

_____

_____

continued

ASSESSMENT CHART: THE NEED FOR ACHIEVEMENT

8. What will happen if I don't "succeed"? How likely is this "disaster fantasy" to occur? Would it really be the end of the world if it did?

Comment:_____

_____

_____

_____

_____

_____

9. What do I want my life-style to be like; what do I want to have accomplished:
   a. 5 years from now?

Comment:_____

_____

_____

_____

_____

_____

_____

   b. 10 years from now?

Comment:_____

_____

_____

_____

_____

_____

_____

   c. 20 years from now?

Comment:_____

_____

_____

_____

_____

_____

continued

ASSESSMENT CHART: THE NEED FOR ACHIEVEMENT

10. a. Write your obituary as it would appear if you died tomorrow.

_____

_____

_____

_____

_____

_____

_____

_____

b. Write your obituary as you hope it would read if you died in the distant future, having made the changes you desire in your life-style and attitude.

_____

_____

_____

_____

_____

_____

_____

_____

_____

_____

THE CONTROL ISSUE: QUESTIONS 9 TO 11. One way in which people differ is the degree to which they believe that what happens to them and *around them* is a result of their behavior. A person who believes that fate or chance decides most events will be unlikely to plan for the future or to give much thought to his or her own behavior, because "after all, what I do doesn't make a difference." In fact, a feeling of loss of control over one's environment has been found to be associated with illness, suicide, and even unexpected death. The adult who says "you (or they) *made* me do it" may be abdicating responsibility for *choosing* to exercise control of his behavior because he fears the consequences of the choice.

The person who believes that everything that happens to him or around him is controlled by or significantly influenced by his actions carries a very heavy responsibility. Much that occurs is beyond our real control. The behavior of our superiors, subordinates, and family may be influenced by us, but we cannot "control" what others do or how they react. Excessive and unrealistic attempts to control all events around us have been found to be associated with a large variety of stress-related diseases and a lowering of resistance to illness in general. A healthy view of the universe would be: "Here are the things I can *influence* and here are the things that are controlled by factors beyond me. The only thing I can *control* is my own behavior. Let me try to *influence* other people and events, but there is no guarantee my attempts can work."

The underlying issue in many people's attempt to maintain control is fear of change or illness and ultimately death. By maintaining the illusion that "I am in control," we can ward off the anxiety of recognizing the uncertainty and ever-changing nature of life, but we only trade that concern for the pressures of trying to "keep the lid on" others and on events. This can lead to poor relations with other people, who appreciate neither our control nor our desperate attempts to manipulate events to meet our needs.

A high score on these questions suggests that you may have an unrealistic view of your personal responsibility for the behavior of others. This places your feelings of competence and responsibility at the mercy of others. You need them to perform to your specifications— otherwise you have failed! This adds unnecessary stress to your life.

If this is a problem area for you, it would be useful for you to think about the following. You can only be responsible for what you do yourself. By your behavior you set up conditions to which others must respond. *How* they respond is a choice that *they* make, even if they want to blame the inevitability of their own choice on *you.* You do not have to accept that argument. You contribute to what happens to you, but you do not control other people.

The concept of problem ownership is useful here. *Whose* life is most directly affected? Who is the person who ultimately must perform actions to change what is happening to him or her? If a subordinate is doing poorly at the job despite your repeated attempts to help, who has the greater problem? Who is more likely to be out of a job? If your daughter is having problems with friends at school, can you *make* the children like her? Can you *make* her be more friendly to others? The point is that you can be concerned about others, try to help, and try to make positive contributions, but the idea that you are personally responsible for finding and implementing a solution for someone else's problem is unrealistic. It may also be harmful to the other person. If you always solve their problems for them, they quickly learn that when there is a problem you will have a solution. In time, this leads to pressure on you to "look good" and to maintain your image by always having an answer. You train people to be unrealistically dependent on you while adding impossible expectations to your role. Stress is the result for you.

This type of problem often shows up on the job in people who are promoted to positions of leadership without adequate management training. Many people have an image of a supervisor as a person who is expected to always have the answers and solve the problems. Unfortunately, this leads to a passive and uncreative staff in which there is poor delegation of all aspects of responsibility.

The problem also appears for the "superparent" or "superfriend" or "superspouse" who feels personally responsible for the behavior and problems of friends and family members. They feel guilty and somehow responsible if others aren't always happy or performing up to expectation.

ASSESSMENT CHART: THE CONTROL ISSUE

Try to answer the following questions. In the work place, training in management or supervisory skills in working with people would be helpful. For parents who feel they should control their children's behavior, many books and courses on parenting offer good advice.

1. On the job, what do I think I am actually supposed to control, not simply to try to influence?

Comment:_____

_____

_____

_____

_____

_____

2. Off the job, what aspects of my life do I think I *should* be able to control?

Comment:_____

_____

_____

_____

_____

_____

_____

3. Other than my own behavior, what in life can I actually control?

Comment:_____

_____

_____

_____

4. What is so frightening about admitting that much of what happens to me and around me is not under my control?

Comment:_____

_____

_____

_____

_____

continued

ASSESSMENT CHART: THE CONTROL ISSUE				

5. Make use of the following chart to assess the control issue in your life in terms of the areas outlined below:

　　a. List the people in your life you want to please.

　　b. For each, indicate if you have ever felt guilty or responsible for disappointing them or not making things better for them or not solving their problems for them. Also indicate for each if *you* ever felt guilty or responsible because *they* let someone else down.

　　c. Indicate for each instance what the problem situation involved objectively.

　　d. For each, was the problem really in your control or your responsibility?

a.	b.	c.	d.	
Name	**Guilt Feelings**	**What Was the Problem Situation?**	**Whose Problem Was It Really?**	
			Yours	**Theirs**

Note: *If control of all aspects of your life is an overriding concern, then professional counseling or therapy would be helpful because you are trying to achieve the unachievable.*

THE WORKAHOLIC SYNDROME: QUESTIONS 12 TO 14.* All employers want hard workers, and all spouses, conscientious partners, but the "workaholic" should be viewed as a mixed blessing, because sooner or later he or she may "burn out." One does not have to be a salaried employee to be a "workaholic." Performing only one role to the exclusion of all others can produce the same results. The self-employed person or the individual who works all the time at being a "superparent" or "superspouse" is subject to the same stresses. A balanced life is generally associated with good health. Even if you are a workaholic who loves your work more than anything else in your life,

---

*Referred to by M. Friedman and R. Rosenman as "Type A" behavior.

putting all your eggs in one basket—be it job, another person, or a specific activity—creates problems if events change. All work and no play suggests a problem in the way a person is ordering his or her life. This can result from feeling competent only in the work (or home) situation, from an overcompensation because of an inadequate social life, or from a retreat from problems in the marriage or family. An excessively high need for achievement or approval can lead to a drive to obtain these goals by excelling at work to the exclusion of all else.

ASSESSMENT CHART: WORKAHOLIC SYNDROME

If your score is high on these questions, then answer the following.

1. Do I really like my work more than anything else in my life?

Comment: _____

_____

_____

2. What else do I enjoy doing other than working?

Comment: _____

_____

_____

3. When was the last time I engaged in these other activities? With what frequency do I engage in them?

Comment: _____

_____

_____

4. Is there something about my values that says work is worthwhile but play is not? If "yes," where did I learn that? Is there a stone tablet on which that commandment is engraved or is it a belief that I have adopted from a parent or relative?

Comment: _____

_____

_____

5. How is my social life? Am I using work to avoid problems I have socializing?

Comment: _____

_____

_____

6. How is my marriage? Am I using work to avoid problems in the marriage? Will they go away if I ignore them?

Comment: _____

_____

_____

_____

continued

ASSESSMENT CHART: WORKAHOLIC SYNDROME

7. How am I getting along with my children or other family members? Am I using work to avoid confronting issues with my family? Will things improve without my presence and involvement?

Comment:_____

_____

_____

_____

8. What would happen if I changed my work habits?

Comment:_____

_____

_____

_____

_____

If being a workaholic seems to be a problem for you and the above questions do not help you to change, then professional counseling would be very helpful.

Health Habits: Stressors

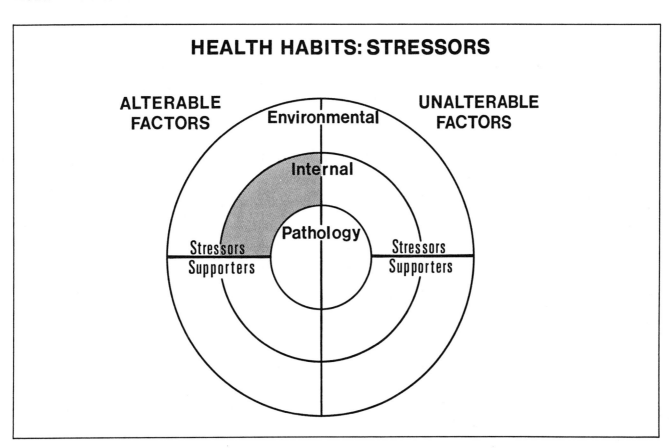

Health Habits: Stressors: *Those behavioral habits which individuals exhibit that tend in themselves to be maladaptive or self-destructive.*

Many of these kinds of behavior, you will recall, are signs of stress. It is interesting to note that many of the signs of stress which we have discussed earlier are in themselves stressful, and in this chapter they will be looked at as stressors in themselves.

HEALTH HABITS: STRESSORS

Overdemanding of others	Reduced food consumption
Overly critical of others	Reduced sleep
Nongiving to others	Hostility
Excessively self-sacrificing	Excessive work
Inability to be constructively assertive	Excessive spending
Poor listening ability	Impulsiveness
Inability to constructively confront others	Recklessness
Inadequate support network	Reduced recreation
Poor decision making	Reduced motion (inertia)
Drug consumption	Inadequate conflict-resolution strategies
Excess food consumption	Others

SCALE 10–HEALTH HABITS: STRESSORS

In order to evaluate your patterns of behavior that might tend to be maladaptive, please complete the following checklist by writing the appropriate number beside the statement given as it applies to the observation, "When I am under stress, I find that I:"

5	4	3	2	1	X
Strongly Agree	**Agree**	**Neutral**	**Disagree**	**Strongly Disagree**	**Do Not Know**

_____ **1.** Increase my alcohol consumption.

Comment: _____

_____ **2.** Increase my food consumption.

Comment: _____

_____ **3.** Increase my coffee consumption.

Comment: _____

continued

5	4	3	2	1	X
Strongly Agree	**Agree**	**Neutral**	**Disagree**	**Strongly Disagree**	**Do Not Know**

_____ **4.** Increase my drug consumption (legal, illegal, prescription, and nonprescription).

Comment: _____

_____

_____ **5.** Become short-tempered.

Comment: _____

_____

_____ **6.** Change my sleeping habits.

Comment: _____

_____

_____ **7.** Spend less time with my family and friends.

Comment: _____

_____

_____ **8.** Work longer hours.*

Comment: _____

_____

_____ **9.** Spend more money than I can afford.

Comment: _____

_____

_____ **10.** Try to change many things in my environment.

Comment: _____

_____

_____ **11.** Smoke more cigarettes.

Comment: _____

_____

_____ **12.** Drive faster.

Comment: _____

_____

_____ **13.** Tend to become reckless.

Comment: _____

_____

_____ **14.** Do less exercise (specific planned exercise).

Comment: _____

_____

_____ **15.** Am less likely to use a seat belt.

Comment: _____

_____

*See discussion on the "workaholic," page 53.

continued

5	4	3	2	1	X
Strongly Agree	Agree	Neutral	Disagree	Strongly Disagree	Do Not Know

_____ **16.** Tend to be less faithful to my spouse.

Comment: _____

_____

_____ **17.** Tend to be less active (more sedentary).

Comment: _____

_____

_____ **18.** Tend to be excessively active, racing about frantically.

Comment: _____

_____

_____ **19.** Become less conscientious, become careless with my work or responsibilities.

Comment: _____

_____

_____ **20.** Tend to annoy those around me.

Comment: _____

_____

_____ **21.** Spend less time relaxing.

Comment: _____

_____

_____ **22.** Spend less time doing the things I enjoy.

Comment: _____

_____

_____ **23.** Fight with people at the slightest provocation, including family and friends.

Comment: _____

_____

_____ **24.** Watch more TV.

Comment: _____

_____

_____ **25.** Other (please specify).

_____ _____

_____ _____

_____ _____

_____ _____

_____ _____

_____ _____

_____ Total

The higher your score, the more likely you are to be jeopardizing your health with your own behavior. As you will recall, these behaviors tend, in themselves, to be stressful and are also signs of stress. See the sections on Chemical Stressors, Diet, Social Stressors, Attitude, and Methods of Increasing Stress Tolerance for specific directions as to how you may deal with your identified problem areas.

Health Habits: Supporters

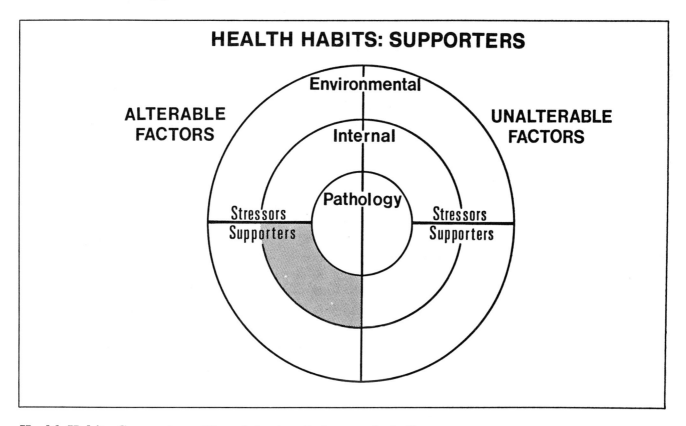

Health Habits: Supporters: *Those behaviors that, as a rule, in themselves tend to be protective or healing; that is, adaptive behavior.*

The supportive behavior may in itself require some effort and be stressful, but the overall effect is positive if done properly. Remember, however, that excesses or extremes of these behaviors that do not match the individual's ability may very well be harmful.

HEALTH HABITS: SUPPORTERS

Altruistic egoism*	Regular exercise	Avoidance of food additives
Constructively assertive	Reasonable food consumption (diet and amount)	Finds satisfaction in varied interests
Ability to be an accurate, nondefensive listener	Use of relaxation techniques and activities	Regular sleep habits
Good communication skills		Adequate conflict-resolution strategies
Adequate support network	Regular visits to trusted health professionals	
Adequate decision-making skills	Avoidance of drugs	

*See Underdemanding/Self-Sacrificing, page 67.

SCALE 11–HEALTH HABITS: SUPPORTERS

In order to evaluate your adaptive behavior patterns, please fill out the following questionnaire using the following scale.

5	4	3	2	1	X
Never	**Rarely**	**Sometimes**	**Frequently**	**Usually**	**Unknown**

_____ **1.** I exercise for 30 minutes at least twice weekly.

Comment: _____

_____

_____ **2.** When I get frustrated I exercise according to recommended guidelines.

Comment: _____

_____

_____ **3.** When I have difficulty with someone, I try to resolve the issue directly and as soon as it is practical.

Comment: _____

_____

_____ **4.** I use some form of relaxation daily.

Comment: _____

_____

_____ **5.** I make it a practice to be nice to people if at all possible.

Comment: _____

_____

_____ **6.** I have a regular family physician with whom I am comfortable and whom I visit at least annually.

Comment: _____

_____

_____ **7.** I make sure my immunizations are up to date.

Comment: _____

_____

_____ **8.** I have a dentist whom I see on a regular basis.

Comment: _____

_____

_____ **9.** If I get angry, either I express it in conversation with the people at whom I am angry or I talk about it with friends.

Comment: _____

_____

_____ **10.** I take out my frustrations when angry on inanimate objects in a safe manner.

Comment: _____

_____

continued

5	4	3	2	1	X
Never	**Rarely**	**Sometimes**	**Frequently**	**Usually**	**Unknown**

11. When I have symptoms which are debilitating or persistent, I visit or talk to my physician.

Comment: _____

12. I talk with a good friend and/or consult a counselor, therapist, or clergyman when confronted with a problem that I'm unable to solve on my own.

Comment: _____

13. I avoid alcohol.

Comment: _____

14. I avoid drugs.

Comment: _____

15. I avoid coffee.

Comment: _____

16. I avoid tea.

Comment: _____

17. I avoid tobacco.

Comment: _____

18. I avoid food additives.

Comment: _____

19. I make an effort to avoid physical, chemical, and biological stressors. If unable to do so, I take precautions in order to minimize their effects.

Comment: _____

20. I take regular vacations.

Comment: _____

21. I have many diversionary interests.

Comment: _____

22. I sleep when I am tired.

Comment: _____

continued

5	4	3	2	1	X
Never	Rarely	Sometimes	Frequently	Usually	Unknown

_____ **23.** I avoid processed foods.

Comment: _____

_____

_____ **24.** I observe the speed limits when driving my car.

Comment: _____

_____

_____ **25.** I wear seat belts when driving or riding in a car.

Comment: _____

_____

_____ **26.** I avoid fat in my diet.

Comment: _____

_____

_____ **27.** I lock up my guns and my ammunition.

Comment: _____

_____

_____ **28.** I pace myself by trying to set enough time aside for what I need to do.

Comment: _____

_____

_____ **29.** I eat fresh fruits and vegetables.

Comment: _____

_____

_____ **30.** I avoid table salt.

Comment: _____

_____

_____ **31.** I am aware of and use appropriate first aid measures when necessary.

Comment: _____

_____

_____ **32.** Other (please list)

_____ _____

_____ _____

Total

The higher the score, the less likely you are to be exhibiting adaptive behavior or behavior which is self-supportive or self-healing. The lower your score, the more likely you are to be exhibiting self-healing behavior. Later on in the book, additional suggestions about how you may change your behavior to promote your health will be discussed (see Implementing Change, Chapter 5).

Interpersonal Style: Stressors

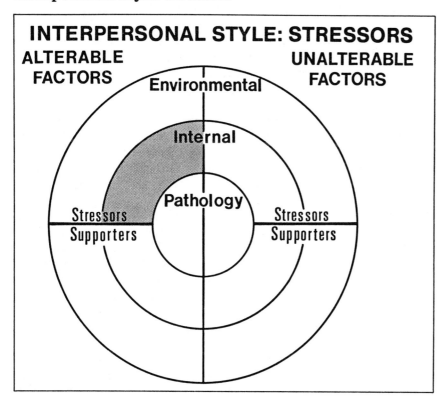

Interpersonal Stressors: *Those behaviors and attitudes concerning relationships that tend to be maladaptive or self-destructive.*

Interpersonal Style: Supporters

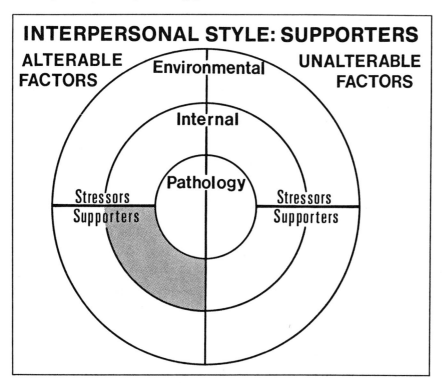

Interpersonal Supporters: *Those behaviors and attitudes concerning relationships that tend to be adaptive or have a healing effect.*

From the viewpoint of the Integrated Model, the following material represents the interaction of the individual's internal attitude and behavior with his social environment.

Dr. Hans Selye, one of the world leaders in stress research, has found that many stress-linked diseases occur in individuals who emphasize either too much *selfishness* in their relationships or too much *self-sacrifice.* Either style influences your relationships with other people. This is important because a critical factor in coping with stress is the support that other people can give you when you are having problems. Friends or relatives can help you sort out your feelings about a problem. They can let you know you are cared for even if other things are going poorly. They may actually be able to suggest a solution to the problem. It is usually more difficult to face pressure alone than with a network of supportive, caring friends and colleagues. This group of family, friends, and co-workers who have some degree of interest in your well-being has been called a person's *support network.*

Your potential support network needs to be nurtured for times when you may need attention or help. If you do not treat people as you would like to be treated, then when you have difficulty they will not be there for you. Dr. Selye calls this "altruistic egoism": look out for yourself by making yourself necessary to others and earning their good will. Without a network of supportive friends, you increase pressure on yourself because you must (1) solve all problems yourself; (2) maintain a position of superiority; (3) do all the work alone; and (4) live in an unsupportive or hostile atmosphere.

On the other hand, we know that persons who live alone tend not to live as long or experience as good health as those who are married or have close relationships with friends or family. Furthermore, poor relationships can produce stress as the expectations and demands of others on you reach uncomfortable limits or as self-imposed isolation promotes depression and more withdrawal.

CHARTING YOUR SUPPORT NETWORK*

The number and quality of your friendships have a direct bearing on your long-term physical and emotional health. This review will help you define the extent and value of your present support network.

A. Friendship means different things to different people. Most people look for friends who are good listeners, who are willing to listen without making judgments about you or forcing their opinion onto you, who are supportive of you and your efforts, who are willing to offer help when needed, and who will be honest with you if they feel you are wrong. List below what qualities you value in a friend:

_____

_____

_____

_____

---

*See Social Supporters, p. 37.

continued

B. List those individuals in your life whom you consider helpful, valuable, or supportive of you.

In Your Personal Life	What Do They Offer You? Why Do You Value Them?	Accessibility (How Easily and Often Can You Talk with Them?)

In Your Work Life (Includes Household Management and Child Care)	What Do They Offer You? Why Do You Value Them?	Accessibility (How Easily and Often Do You Talk with Them?)

C. Now go back to B and check those people who are geographically accessible to you.
D. Review this material. What conclusions can you draw about the adequacy of your support network? Is it large enough? Are there enough people geographically near you? Are there any surprising entries or absences on your lists? Indicate below any deficiencies you have found in your support network and what you think you should do about strengthening it.

Changes Necessary in My Personal Support System	Excuses I Will Make to Avoid Making These Changes

continued

Changes Necessary in My Work Support System	Excuses I Will Make to Avoid Making These Changes
_____	_____
_____	_____
_____	_____
_____	_____
_____	_____
_____	_____

In contrast to a written outline characterizing your support network, the simplification of a visual representation can also be a valuable device.

DIAGRAMMING YOUR SOCIAL ENVIRONMENT

In the circle below, place the names of all friends, colleagues, and relatives you consider part of your network. Place them in the circle in proximity to your name according to who you believe would be most likely to really extend himself to you if you needed help or support. The closer to the center, the more certain you are of their help and support.

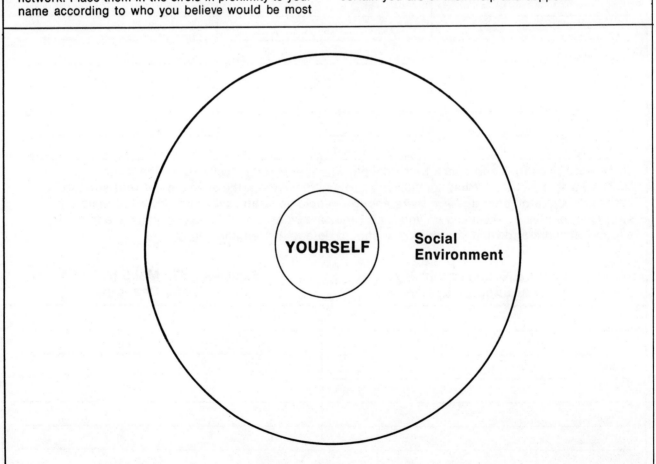

Stressful Interpersonal Styles

OVERDEMANDING/NONGIVING (SELFISHNESS). The issues are clear. If you demand a great deal from others but do not reciprocate in kind, they will be much less willing to take care of you when you are in need. If you dispense mainly criticism and little praise, recognition, or love, you will receive back only what you have put out.

This style is common among people whose high need for personal achievement overrides the needs and feelings of the people around them. It often occurs in people with a high need to control the behavior of those around them, for example, managers, parents, or spouses who believe that leadership means ordering the "troops" about from task to task without concern for their feelings. These individuals may be operating from feelings of superiority or inferiority, saying, in effect, "I can do this better than anyone, so why even involve them; I'll do it my way alone rather than risk being refused if I ask for help," or "I must always be right or I'll lose respect."

Another problem with a leadership or parenting style that calls for always having the best answer regardless of the underlying motive is that those under you quickly lose their initiative and their willingness to share ideas with you or to try out their own ideas. They may become quietly hostile and resistant. They may come to depend on you to have the answer in all situations. This in turn places considerable pressure on you because now you *do* have to be right all the time and others will accept nothing less from you. If you can delegate responsibility comfortably, you can admit you do not know everything, that the right way is not always your way, and that others in the organization or family have valuable contributions to make, then you avoid this particular trap. Spouses who try to impose this autocratic style on their partners run a high risk of an unhappy marriage or divorce if the partner is not comfortable in a "subordinate" position.

UNDERDEMANDING/SELF-SACRIFICING (THE "MARTYR"). People who act like doormats assume this role because they fear they have nothing else to offer but their services as requested. Often individuals with a very high need for approval will try to gain that approval by doing whatever is asked of them regardless of whether they want to or not. The fear of disapproval if they say "no" motivates them to take on tasks that cause them inconvenience, hardship, and frustration. Such individuals may become workaholics. Others may become the person everyone takes advantage of because they have broadcast their availability for that role to those around them.

For the sacrificing individual, this role inevitably leads to a circular trap. Martyrs at some point become angry at others for taking advantage of them and angry at themselves for always doing what others want; but since their main goal is *approval*, they can't risk showing their anger. When they begin to sense their anger, they become anxious and often depressed. The circle is then complete: "To gain approval, I cannot say no. By saying yes, I wind up not leading my own life. Not leading my own life makes me angry. To show anger risks disapproval. I had better hide my anger, even from myself, and do what is asked of me and not say no."

Some individuals may use this style as a manipulative strategy to "control" others by inducing guilt. If those around such an individual are reasonably sensitive, considerate people, it is difficult for them to refuse someone who is always sacrificing his or her time and energy for them. For example, the caricatured "Martyred Mother" may actually think quite highly of herself, but learned when she was growing up that women get what they want from others by giving, not requesting. She gives and gives and gives until others feel *obligated* to deny her nothing. The resultant frustration, annoyance, and anger cannot be expressed to such a "saint," so the others feel guilty. The underlying stress in such relationships can make both parties unhappy—if not physically ill.

SCALE 12–BEHAVIORAL STRESSORS: INTERPERSONAL STYLE

Below are a number of questions which will help you assess how much you demand from other people.

Rate your answers from 5 to 1 according to how frequently the experiences described happen to you.

5	4	3	2	1
Always	**Often**	**Sometimes**	**Rarely**	**Never**

OVER-DEMANDING/ NONGIVING

_____ **1.** I demand more from others than I return.

Comment: _____

_____

_____ **2.** I am told I criticize much more than I praise.

Comment: _____

_____

_____ **3.** I believe that people work best when they are pushed and continually told what to do rather than when given responsibility and left on their own.

Comment: _____

_____

_____ **4.** I believe that I should be able to solve all the problems brought to me.

Comment: _____

_____

_____ **5.** I do not admit I know less than a subordinate or my spouse, because I am afraid I will lose their respect or my power over them.

Comment: _____

_____

_____ Total

continued

5	4	3	2	1
Always	**Often**	**Sometimes**	**Rarely**	**Never**
UNDER-DEMANDING/ SELF-SACRIFICING				

_____ **1.** I am reluctant to ask others for the time I freely give them.

Comment: _____

_____

_____ **2.** Others tell me I am too self-sacrificing.

Comment: _____

_____

_____ **3.** I feel I do not deserve to ask for time and effort from others.

Comment: _____

_____

_____ **4.** I feel I work too hard and take too little time for myself.

Comment: _____

_____

_____ **5.** Others tell me I tend to work too hard and take too little time for myself.

Comment: _____

_____

_____ **6.** I get angry when other people do not help me the way I help them, but I usually do not say anything.

Comment: _____

_____

_____
Total

If your score is high, the usual cure for these types of stress-inducing styles is the development of a stronger, more broadly based self-esteem. If you are too self-sacrificing, popular books on being more assertive and community assertiveness-training programs can be helpful. If you are too demanding, you may either be overcompensating for a low self-image and trying to play "tough," or you may believe you are superior to those around you. If you control others through guilt manipulation, you may have limited flexibility in how you learned to relate to people. In any case, your relationships will suffer considerably and professional counseling may be very helpful.

Behavioral Stressors:

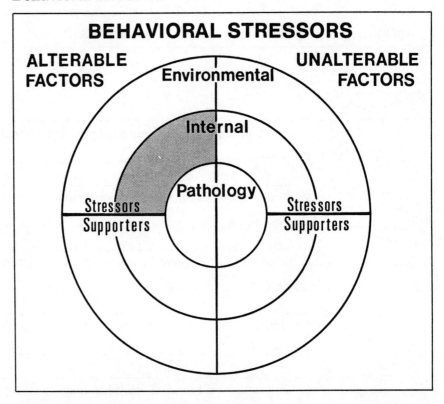

Stressful Communication: *Means of communication, verbal and nonverbal, that tend to be maladaptive or self-destructive.*

Behavioral Supporters:

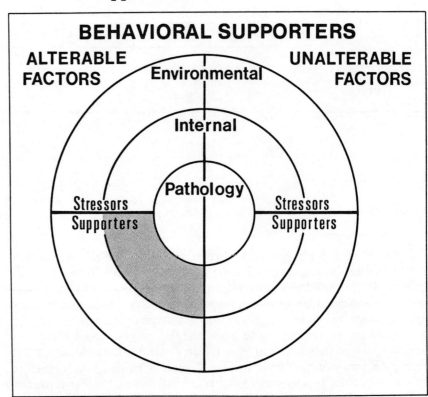

Stressors—Maladaptive or Self-Defeating

Inability to be constructively assertive

Poor listening ability

Inability to constructively confront others

Inability to respond to and express emotions

Supporters—Adaptive or Self-Constructive

Constructively assertive

Ability to be an accurate, nondefensive listener

Ability to constructively confront others

Ability to express emotions

Supportive Communication: *Means of communication, verbal and nonverbal, that tend to be adaptive or self-healing.*

Your ability to express yourself influences the amount of stress in your relationships and how well you can get assistance from others in coping with your problems. The inability to express your feelings or intellectual opinions clearly or the inability to confront an issue constructively can lead to the type of friction that is often labeled "personality problems." Good communication is a skill. The better your ability to communicate becomes, the more comfortable you will be.

SCALE 13–INTERNAL BEHAVIORAL STRESSORS: COMMUNICATION SKILLS

Below is a checklist that will help you assess your strengths and weaknesses in communicating with others. Mark each item twice, first with your assessment of yourself and then with what you think others would say about you. Think about what other people have said about you and how they act with you, and make an honest guess about their feelings. Better still, ask some trusted friends or colleagues to fill out a copy of this inventory with their impressions of you.

5	4	3	2	1
I Always Do This/Others Always See Me This Way	I Often Do This/ Others Often See Me This Way	I Sometimes Do This/Others Sometimes See Me This Way	I Rarely Do This/Others Rarely See Me This Way	I Never Do This/Others Never See Me This Way

HOW I SEE MYSELF	HOW OTHERS SEE ME	
_____	_____	**1.** People tell me I am a good listener. They feel good talking with me. Comment: _____
_____	_____	**2.** Others tell me I misunderstand what they are trying to say, that talking with me is often frustrating. Comment: _____
_____	_____	**3.** I seem to have difficulty getting others to understand my point of view. I often end up feeling misunderstood. Comment: _____
_____	_____	**4.** Others tell me that they avoid talking to me because my mind often seems made up beforehand and they feel/know I will not change. Comment: _____

continued

5	4	3	2	1
I Always Do This/Others Always See Me This Way	**I Often Do This/ Others Often See Me This Way**	**I Sometimes Do This/Others Sometimes See Me This Way**	**I Rarely Do This/Others Rarely See Me This Way**	**I Never Do This/Others Never See Me This Way**

HOW I SEE MYSELF	HOW OTHERS SEE ME			

———————   ———————

5. I avoid talking with others about their feelings and emotional issues and/or try to change the subject or distract them if they become upset.

Comment: _____

_____

_____

_____

———————   ———————

6. I avoid talking with others about my feelings about them, about the situation in general.

Comment: _____

_____

_____

_____

———————   ———————

———————   ———————

7. If someone has let me down or not done his or her job, I:
   a. say nothing but feel upset.

   b. try to let him or her know indirectly—through others, sarcasm, etc..

Comment: _____

_____

_____

_____

———————   ———————

———————   ———————

8. When I am angry, I tend to blow my stack:

   a. at the individual who upset me.

   b. at whomever is around.

Comment: _____

_____

_____

_____

———————   ———————

9. If someone is angry with me, I tend to get defensive and angry rather than try to listen to his or her viewpoint.

Comment: _____

_____

_____

_____

continued

5	4	3	2	1
I Always Do This/Others Always See Me This Way	**I Often Do This/ Others Often See Me This Way**	**I Sometimes Do This/Others Sometimes See Me This Way**	**I Rarely Do This/Others Rarely See Me This Way**	**I Never Do This/Others Never See Me This Way**

HOW I SEE MYSELF	HOW OTHERS SEE ME	
————	————	**10.** What else do your family, colleagues, or friends say about your style of listening and dealing with feelings and making yourself clearly understood?
		Comment: _____
		_____
		_____
		_____
		_____
		_____
		_____
		_____
		_____
		_____
		_____
		_____
		_____
		_____
————	————	_____
Total	Total	

Communication Barriers and Distortion

Your listening is particularly poor when you are emotionally aroused, feel threatened or anxious, or feel there is a great deal at stake in your conversation. The reason for this is that we all have a tendency to see and hear what we expect to see and hear. We select from all the hundreds of cues around us at a given moment, those cues that are important to us at the time and pay attention to just those. That is called *selective attention* or *selective perception*. Furthermore, we tend to distort those cues we do pay attention to so that they fit our preconceived idea of what is "supposed" to happen. For example, if you believe you are not liked, you will ignore or distort other peoples' overtures to you to conform to your expectation that they will not be approving, interested, friendly, etc. This is called *perceptual distortion*. Therefore, reality is only what you interpret it to be from the cues you choose to pay attention to. You scan your surroundings to locate evidence that people are feeling and behaving as you expect, even if their behavior is not to your liking. You tend to distort or ignore evidence that does not conform to what you expect. You must develop humility about the accuracy of your perceptions of others' motives. Unless you are telepathic, you cannot read minds and will often be in error. Look at the following diagram.

INTENDED MESSAGE	POSSIBLE INTERPRETATIONS	RECEIVED MESSAGE
"Let's talk. I want to be friendly by expressing interest in you."	1. How are you feeling physically? 2. How are you feeling emotionally? 3. "Let's talk." Simple recognition, no response expected. 4. Sarcasm: "Have you recovered from the awful presentation you made last night?" 5. (How many others can you think of?)	Superficial greeting, no response expected.
OUTCOME	**POSSIBLE OUTCOMES**	**OUTCOME**
"This guy is not interested in me—I guess I'll stay away from him."	1. This guy is unfriendly. 2. He is not interested in me. 3. He is not outgoing enough to fit into this organization. 4. He must have a problem he is worried about. 5. I wonder if he is angry at me. 6. (How many others can you think of?)	She is not interested in me—I'll stay away from her.

To complicate the matter further, less than half of what we communicate is transmitted by words. The remainder is sent through nonverbal channels such as our tone of voice, our body posture, and the *timing* of what we say ("I wonder why he said that to me just after she showed up rather than doing it before she came?"). When there seems to be a discrepancy between the verbal message and the nonverbal message, we tend to give credence to the nonverbal aspect. This is what is referred to as "vibrations" or "intuition." The problem is that nonverbal messages are even more ambiguous than verbal communication. Often you are not aware of the nonverbal cues you are receiving. You cannot easily check them out, therefore, even if you are comfortable doing so.

INTENDED VERBAL MESSAGE	POSSIBLE INTERPRETATIONS	RECEIVED NONVERBAL MESSAGES
"Let's get down to work."	1. "This is acceptable work. You did OK." 2. "You're in trouble. I don't like your work." 3. "I am ready to review your work on this project."	"I thought this was routine but he looks annoyed. He's frowning. What have I done wrong?"
NONVERBAL CUE "This headache is killing me."		

You can deal with this difficulty by paying attention to your "vibrations" or feelings and checking them out when you think you are receiving a confused or double message. Referring back to the last diagram, you can say, "From your expression, I have the impression that you are not pleased with my report," to which the response could be, "No, the report is fine, but my head is killing me."

PARAPHRASING. Paraphrasing is a basic technique that usually overcomes problems of selective and distorted perceptions. It is used to check your perceptions of the other person's meaning and intentions. Basically, if you want to know if you are interpreting someone accurately, *ask* the person. Paraphrasing means taking *your* interpretation of the other person's words and/or actions, putting them into *your own words,* and then *asking* the other person if your assumptions are accurate. This technique is the foundation for good communication skills and for many counseling approaches. For example, a wife is sitting at the breakfast table with her husband. The following dialogue occurs without the use of paraphrasing.

WIFE: "What do you think about having the Smiths over for dinner?"

HUSBAND: "Just when am I supposed to find the time to finish that project you keep nagging me about?"

WIFE: "At the rate you finish things, our friends would all be dead before you have a free evening to socialize."

HUSBAND: "You aren't the most efficient person I know either. What about that mending you were supposed to do last month?"

WIFE: "If I had some more help with the children, I'd have time to do your mending."

HUSBAND: "If you paid more attention to your responsibilities and less time watching TV, things would run better around here."

Note the problems these people are getting into because they are not checking out their assumptions before getting defensive and attacking each other. If paraphrasing is used to make sure interpretations are correct, more constructive problem solving usually follows and many unnecessary fights can be avoided (the paraphrasing is underlined):

WIFE: "What do you think about having the Smiths over for dinner?"

HUSBAND: "Are you suggesting we have them over tonight?"

WIFE: "Not necessarily. I was just thinking it would be nice to get together with them soon. Are you saying tonight would be bad timing for you?"

HUSBAND: "Yes. You have been pushing me to finish that project and I thought I would work on it tonight."

WIFE: "You sound frustrated about that. Did you think I was angry you haven't finished it yet?"

HUSBAND: "Sure. You always sound annoyed when you ask about it."

WIFE: "Well, I wouldn't say I've felt annoyed. I know you've been busy with other things. I'm just anxious to have that finished so we can get into the next project. That's the one I am really excited about."

HUSBAND: "I'm glad you are not annoyed. I get uncomfortable when you are angry. But how come if you are so anxious for me to finish, you keep thinking up other things for us to do in the evenings?"

WIFE: "I guess I do get impatient when you're working at home, when I'd rather be out with our friends. Why don't we set aside two evenings for you to work on that project and two evenings to play each week until the whole thing is done?"

HUSBAND: "OK, let's try that."

Paraphrasing is not a cure-all. There are circumstances where it will not always be helpful; and many people don't always use it correctly. Common problems in using paraphrasing include *parroting, overuse,* and *playing amateur psychiatrist.*

Parroting means using the other person's words verbatim; it sounds phony, contrived, and generally makes the other person annoyed or angry, for example:

WIFE: "Dammit, leave me alone."

HUSBAND: "You want me to leave you alone?"

WIFE: "Yes. Leave me alone. I am too angry to talk with you now."

HUSBAND: "You are too angry to talk now?"

WIFE: "Damn right. Now go away."

HUSBAND: "You want me to go away?"

Obviously, this is an absurd way to respond, but some people believe this is paraphrasing. It is the type of attempt that gives paraphrasing a bad name. Look at the use of real paraphrasing (underlined below):

WIFE: "Dammit, leave me alone."

HUSBAND: "Are you really saying you don't want to try to talk this out?"

WIFE: "No. I'll feel more like talking later. Right now, I want privacy."

HUSBAND: "OK. Do you want me to come back later or will you find me?"

WIFE: "I'll find you. Now leave me alone."

HUSBAND: "OK. I didn't realize you prefer to be alone when you are really angry."

WIFE: "I don't always. Just this time."

HUSBAND: "I thought you were saying I should always stay away when you are upset."

WIFE: "No. That would create more problems. Just give me some room right now."

HUSBAND: "OK. I'll be ready to talk when you are."

Overuse of paraphrasing is a common mistake among people attempting to become comfortable with the approach. Notice in the above examples that the paraphrasing is interspersed with other comments, problem-solving suggestions, etc. It is helpful to use paraphrasing when you want to make certain of your observations. It is one of a number of different ways that people talk with each other, not something to be done all the time.

The *amateur psychiatrist* trap is one that often befalls someone who has taken a psychology or communications course or has read a book on that subject. The amateur psychiatrist will interpret others' thoughts and motives for them unsolicited. People will often resent someone else telling them what they think or feel. It presumes that you can read between the lines and accurately guess what another person's *real* motive and feelings are even if not expressed. It is important to remember that paraphrasing is a *guess*. You are using your own words to describe what you *think* you are hearing and seeing. As long as you put a question mark at the end of your paraphrase, it is less likely that the other person will take offense. The final variable in the degree of success of paraphrasing is the *other person*. That person may not always react to paraphrasing the way you wish. If you get an unexpected response, try finding out what the other person *thought* you said. Ask the individual to paraphrase you, for example: "Wait a moment before you get upset. I may not have expressed myself clearly. What did you think I said?" In the end, all you can do is play the odds. The odds are that your communication will be clearer and involve fewer misunderstandings if you paraphrase when:

1. Emotions (yours, theirs, or both) are aroused, which is when perceptual distortion is highest.

2. You or they are unclear about what the communication means.

3. A lot of material is being discussed and it is hard to remember everything.

4. You want to periodically summarize and let the other person know you are trying hard to listen.

Here is an exercise you can do with a friend, spouse, or colleague that will help you to improve your ability to be a good listener and practice paraphrasing.

LISTENING EXERCISE

1. Choose a topic that has emotional involvement for at least one if not both of you. (Perceptual distortion will be greatest then.)

2. Take turns discussing your point of view and your *feelings* (emotions) about the topic.

3. One person at a time has the floor. The other person must sit, listen, and not interrupt. The speaker can say anything about the topic she or he wishes.

4. Before the listener can respond with her or his own ideas and feelings, she or he must *earn* the right to do so.

5. To earn the right to respond, the listener now must paraphrase the speaker to the speaker's satisfaction. The listener now uses her or his own words to tell the speaker what the listener *thought* she or he heard the speaker say.

6. *If* the speaker is satisfied that he or she has been understood, *then* the listener can become the speaker and talk about her or his feelings and opinions and the other person now listens without interrupting.

7. When the new speaker is finished, the new listener must then paraphrase to the speaker's satisfaction in order to earn the right to respond.

8. The conversation continues back and forth this way, with each listener earning the right to respond by paraphrasing.

9. If the speaker does not feel adequately understood (paraphrased), she or he repeats the points of contention, allowing the listener as many opportunities as necessary to paraphrase correctly.

Ten to twenty minutes of this exercise will make you very sensitive to your style of listening and speaking. You will find yourself making two mistakes throughout this exercise.

First, as a listener, you will spend time *thinking ahead* to what you want to say when your turn comes and, consequently, not listening to the speaker. This is because we tend to be competitive in our conversations, our goal being to "win," not necessarily to understand. We "win" when we convert the other person to our point of view. Therefore, what they have to say is important only to find loopholes we may use to weaken their argument and win them over. This is fine for a debate but makes for poor understanding and bad feelings in relationships. Try "understanding," not "winning," as a goal. You don't have to agree in order to understand. And if you do understand, you can formulate a more useful argument *if* "winning" is your goal. Finally, good listening really helps the other person feel good. People like to be listened to and rarely have the experience. You will reap many benefits in your relationships if you have a reputation for being a "good listener." (Research indicates that being a good listener is considered by many to be one of the major criteria for friendship in our society.)

Second, when you are the speaker, you will find you are often paraphrased in a far briefer manner than you spoke. You may talk too much because (1) you haven't thought out your ideas before speaking; and (2) if you don't see the other person responding, you assume they don't understand and so you repeat yourself again and again and again. It will be easier for others to understand you if you present the material briefly, or a little at a time, and ask for paraphrasing to make certain you are understood before you continue.

CONSTRUCTIVE CONFRONTING. The second major communication skill needed is the ability to confront another person *constructively* when that person's behavior has had an impact on you. Most of us do not deal well with our anger or with being direct with others about things they might not want to hear. We seem to be afraid that any direct communication like this will inevitably result in hurt feelings, anger or, alienation, a worse situation. If we were honest with ourselves, we would also admit that we avoid such directness because we fear that to establish such a precedent in a relationship would mean that the other person might then confront us. In many of our relationships, we have made an unspoken agreement to be less than honest with each other. The difficulty with this approach is that problems do not get resolved. The resulting feelings of annoyance, frustration, anger, or guilt create stress. The longer the situation remains unresolved, the worse the stress can become. Our perceptions then become influenced by our discomfort, and we may make the situation worse by making erroneous interpretations about the other person's motives. A minority of people take a different approach to confrontation. They attack and belittle others and use sarcasm and inflammatory labels to describe other people's character and motivation. Reasons for this style can be found in the preceding material on attitude and overdemanding interpersonal style. Regardless of the reason, this approach can be devastating to others and very destructive of relationships.

The most constructive way to deal directly with a sensitive issue is to:

1. Talk with a close friend about the *behavior* in question and how the behavior affects you.

2. Not assume you know the person's motive for behaving.

3. Indicate that you want to talk about the problem in order to improve the relationship, not to hurt, punish, score points, etc.

4. Talk about the situation as soon as possible so it is fresh in everybody's mind.

5. Not use inflammatory or derogatory labels to describe the other person's behavior or motives.

6. Be specific about what bothers you. Talk about the other person's *behavior,* not assumed motives.

7. Give examples.

8. *Not try to "win."* Try to understand the other person's perspective; help him or her see yours without feeling competitive. A solution will emerge when you understand each other.

The material available on communication skills is enormous. The basic principles are the same regardless of the specific method taught. A comprehensive training program in good communication is beyond the scope of this workbook. However, written material can be found in any bookstore, and workshops in communication skills are readily available from many sources.

There are ways of verbally structuring your confrontations to lessen the chances the other person will feel attacked and consequently become defensive and counterattack. These methods are not foolproof, but they do substantially raise the odds of a constructive or, at least, nondestructive outcome.

Direct Feedback

The "feedback" or "confrontation" approach most heavily popularized in recent years involves three basic pieces of information: the other person's specific behavior that you are reacting to, your emotional reaction to that behavior, and a reason for your reaction. The structure looks like this:

I feel *(your emotion)* when you *(specific behavior by the other person),* because *(reason for your reaction).*

The order can be rearranged and different words substituted. The words are not magic. What is important are the three basic ingredients that provide enough information for the other person to know how to change if they wish to and/or how their behavior will affect you if they choose not to change. For example:

A. "John, *I am* really upset *when you* promise to be home for supper at a particular time and then you don't call when you are late. *Then,* I am left with crying, hungry kids, not knowing whether to serve dinner without you. At the end of the day, I can't handle the frustration well."

B. "Mary, *when* you promise to have a report to me on a specific date and then don't deliver it, *I get* put in a compromising position with my superiors, who are waiting for it. That *makes me* angry with you and defensive with them."

Notice that in both examples, neither John nor Mary is attacked, labeled, called disparaging names, etc. It is their *behavior* that is the problem, not them as people. John and Mary can deal more easily with problems their behavior causes than they can with personal attacks on their character. Notice the difference below.

A. "John, I'm sick and tired of your *selfish lack of consideration.* You *never think of us. If you loved your family,* you'd be home for supper or you'd call."

B. "Mary, you are *irresponsible* and *lazy.* We'll have to find a replacement for you if you can't act more reliably."

The personal attacks and assumptions about underlying motives in the second set of examples are likely to produce only bad feelings, defensiveness, or worse. Even if the assumptions are true, which in most cases they are not, the possibility for constructively reaching a compromise is diminished by such an approach. People are tempted to blow off steam like this when they have been sitting on their feelings for some time, hoping the problem would go away. When they finally deal with it, they blow sky high. This is another reason for dealing with issues as they arise and are still of manageable size. Also, it is much easier for people to successfully paraphrase someone who is not attacking them.

After stating your feelings about the other person's behavior, *keep quiet and listen* to his or her response. *Check your perception* about his or her response before deciding what to do next. You and the other person should paraphrase your positions and feelings for a few minutes *before* trying to compromise or decide to give up on each other.

There are times when the other person seems to contradict himself or herself in some way that is important to you, him or her, or both of you. The person may say one thing and then contradict that at a later time: "Of course my family comes first, but I have an obligation to my company to work nights and weekends if necessary to do the job they expect of me." They may say one thing and do the opposite: "Sure, I'll help my spouse with the housework and the kids," but there is no behavioral follow-through. They may do one thing and then do the opposite later: Bill gets some of his reports in on time to his supervisor, but many others are late. These contradictions can be dealt with through paraphrasing the contradictions as well as by using the "I feel ———" approach outlined above. Before saying anything, identify the discrepancies you *think* you see. Then consider the following approaches.

1. *Confusion Approach*

"Cheryl, I am confused. You tell me that the kids and I come first with you, but since you got that job you work whenever your boss asks you to, including nights, weekends, holidays, and my birthday. What's going on?" *or*

"Sam, I'm getting confused about our agreement. You promised to help with the housework and the kids, but you always have something else scheduled when I tell you I need your help. Did I misunderstand your commitment to help me?" *or*

"Bill, I'm not clear on what you are doing with your work time. Sometimes you're prompt and sometimes you're very late. What is going on to produce such erratic results in your production?"

2. *Summarizing Approach*

"Let me see if I understand, Cheryl. I thought you said last time we talked that the kids and I were your first priority. But since that time, you have worked four out of five nights, a whole weekend, and missed my birthday. Is that correct?" *or*

"Sam, before I get angry, I want to make sure we see things the same way. As I remember it, you promised to help whenever I asked you to lend a hand with the kids and the housework. Right? But the first five times I asked after that agreement, you had other commitments. Am I remembering this correctly?" *or*

"Bill, as I recall, you wanted to be recognized as a reliable worker. Yet it is my impression that many of your reports are late. Can you explain to me what is happening?"

You can see that both of these approaches merely summarize or paraphrase the apparent discrepancy. The reason these approaches are useful is that (1) they give you a chance to check your perception of the "apparent discrepancy" before proceeding (you both may be operating on different assumptions); and (2) it is harder for a defensive person to attack someone who is asking for help ("I'm confused") or just summarizing the *behavioral* facts ("Let's see if I remember correctly"). You want them to focus on the discrepancy, not get sidetracked on defending themselves against personal labels; for example, whether Sam is lazy or not is not the issue. Whether he has his reports in on time is the issue.

The Third Person Approach

Sometimes the other individual may be too defensive to hear directly about himself, or you have a guess about his or her motivations but are not certain. You can soften the impact of the confrontation and/or protect yourself if your guess is wrong by prefacing your remarks with an illustration of an *unnamed or imaginary third party*. For example, suppose you notice that a colleague tends to routinely work much longer than required hours even though he talks about problems that his children are experiencing in school and at home. You might wonder why he chooses to work over time while also complaining about his children's difficulties. You could ask him, "I've been wondering, Bill. *Sometimes people* around here work longer hours when things get tough at home so they have a good reason not to have to tackle those problems. I've been wondering if that's happening to you these days?"

By introducing a "third" party, you might relieve the stigma some people would feel at admitting to a problem. If "others" feel or behave that way it may be easier for them to acknowledge their feelings and motives to you.

This is also an excellent approach to use with children who may not realize their feelings and motives until labeled for them and/or who fears disapproval or stigma if admitting to hidden feelings. For example, "You know, Mary, *many boys and girls* worry that they have personally done something to cause their parents to divorce. I wonder if you have been worried about that since your father and I separated?"

CONFRONTATION EXERCISE

List two or more people whose behavior is (or has been) a problem for you. Describe the specific behavior, how it makes you feel and why it is a problem.	Then write up a confrontation using the model provided. If you want to expand on this you can use a separate sheet of paper.

Situation 1

A. The person is: _____

_____

B. The behavior I have a problem with is: _____

_____

_____

C. The situation(s) in which that behavior is a problem: _____

_____

_____

D. The reason that behavior is a problem for me in that situation(s): _____

_____

_____

E. The emotions I feel when confronted with this problem behavior are: _____

_____

_____

F. _____ , I feel _____
　　(Person's name)　　　　　　　　　　　　　(specific emotion)

when you _____
　　　　　(specific behavior)

_____

_____

because _____
　　　　　(reason for your feelings)

_____

_____

continued

Situation 2

A. The person is: _____
_____

B. The behavior I have a problem with is:
_____
_____

C. The situation(s) in which that behavior is a problem:
_____
_____

D. The reason that behavior is a problem for me in those situation(s):
_____
_____

E. The emotions I feel when confronted with this problem behavior are:
_____

F. _____ , I feel _____
    (Person's name)   *(specific emotion)*

when you _____
        (specific behavior)
_____

because _____
      (reason for your feelings)
_____

Now, list two or more people whose behavior (verbal and/or nonverbal) presents apparent discrepancies.

Then write two confrontations using the models provided below.

Situation 1

A. The person is: _____
_____
_____

B. The apparent contradiction is that _____
                                                (name)

says or does _____
_____ ,

but then he or she also says or does _____
_____
_____ .

C. _____ , I am confused when you _____
    (Person's name)
_____ and then
_____ .

continued

D. _____ , as I see it, you said (or did) _____
(Person's name)

_____ ,

but then _____ .

Is that correct?

E. _____ , sometimes people will _____
(Person's name)   *(state contradiction)*

_____

when they _____ .
       (state your guess about their motives)

_____

Could that be true for you?

Situation 2

A. The person is: _____

_____

B. The apparent contradiction is that _____
                                            (name)

says or does _____

_____ ,

but then he or she also says or does _____

_____ .

C. _____ , I am confused when you _____
(Person's name)

_____ and then

_____ .

D. _____ , as I see it, you said (or did) _____
(Person's name)

_____ ,

but then _____ .

Is that correct?

E. _____ , sometimes people will _____
(Person's name)   *(state contradiction)*

_____

when they _____
       (state your guess about their motives)

_____

Could that be true for you?

Problem Solving

Remember that these approaches to communication do not guarantee a successful outcome. They do, however, significantly increase the chances of a constructive, or at least nondestructive, encounter. After your opening remark in a confrontation, wait and listen. Hear the other person's response. Ask that person to paraphrase you. When you are hearing each other accurately, *many apparent conflicts disappear.* If the conflict remains, then you can try to negotiate.

Negotiation means that each of you gets *part* of what you want. Try to look for common ground first: Where do you agree? Next, look for areas of potential compromise. If you insist that one side must "win" and the other "lose," the conflict cannot be eliminated. On areas where neither of you can find a middle ground you can live with, decide how you will continue to live or work together agreeing to disagree on these issues.

One good way to negotiate is through "brainstorming." List all the ideas you can think of, silly or not, that might help you with the problem. (Sometimes the "silly" ones are the most creative.) Just list them all without critique. Criticizing at this stage drives "weird" (but creative) ideas underground. Select from that list the ones you agree might work. Next, take them one at a time, in an order on which you both agree, and decide how to implement the idea. Try it out and agree on a time to talk about how it is working out. If there are problems, negotiate an answer to the problems. If that doesn't work, try the next solution on the brainstorm list. Remember, if your mutual goal is to try to live or work together, then you will be able to live amicably even with some differences.

PROBLEM-SOLVING EXERCISE

Choose a person with whom you have or have had a disagreement. If they are available, do this exercise together. State the problem. List at least 10 possible solutions, regardless of their reasonableness. Then eliminate ones that seem unproductive. From the ones remaining, choose the solution you would like to try first. How would you implement it? Who would do what, when, where, and how? When would you review your progress?

The person is: _____

_____

The problem is: _____

_____

_____

What did you try? _____

_____

_____

Why did it not work? _____

_____

continued

Whose problem is it really? (Yours? Theirs? Shared?) _____

_____

What do I want from this person? (More? Less? Same?)* _____

_____

List at least 10 different things that you could try. Check any expectations that might be unreasonable.

1. _____   6. _____
2. _____   7. _____
3. _____   8. _____
4. _____   9. _____
5. _____   10. _____

*For an expansion on this, see Item 1 under Role-Based Stress, p. 99.

List these brainstorming solutions in order of preference:

	YOURS	THEIRS	SHARED
1.			
2.			
3.			
4.			
5.			
6.			
7.			
8.			
9.			
10.			

Which one will you try first?

Who will do what? _____

      when? _____

     where? _____

      how? _____

When will you meet to review your progress? _____

What excuses will you use to avoid following these recommendations? _____

_____

_____

Dealing with Someone Who Is Angry

Many people have a lot of difficulty knowing how to react constructively to someone who is angry. The fear of expressed anger is a major motivator for people not being open about their feelings and opinions. We often assume that anger is always bad or destructive. This is not so. Anger is neither good nor bad. It is the consequences of the anger that determine whether an incident is constructive or destructive. Expressions of anger can blow off steam, defuse tension, and lead to problem solving if handled well. Dealing with your anger through the confrontation approaches described on preceding pages will alleviate many of the "explosive" kinds of situations people fear. Sometimes we encounter someone who is emotionally very upset. The best way to deal with physically abusive persons is to leave the situation until they calm down to the point where they are not dangerous. Most people, however, are verbally aggressive when expressing anger.

Please fill out the following Anger Exercise, the goal of which is to help you become aware of your usual interpersonal style of dealing with angry people in your life.

ANGER EXERCISE

When someone is angry at me, I feel: _____
_____

When someone is angry at me, I tend to behave in the following way:_____
_____

When someone is angry in my presence about a friend or issue I have emotional attachments to, I feel:_____

When someone is angry in my presence about a friend or issue I have emotional attachments to, I tend to behave: _____

When someone is angry in my presence about someone or some issue I have no emotional attachments to, I feel: _____

When someone is angry in my presence about someone or some issue I have no emotional attachments to, I tend to behave: _____
_____

Describe two or more situations involving someone being angry in your presence: (1) about you, (2) about someone or something other than you. How did you handle it and how could you have done it differently?

Situation 1 (Angry about you)

  A. The person is: _____

  B. The issue was:_____
_____

continued

C. I said and did the following: _____

_____

_____

_____

D. If I were to have a second chance, I would say and do the following: _____

_____

_____

_____

_____

Situation 2 (Angry about someone/something other than you)

   A. The person is: _____

   B. The issue was: _____

_____

_____

   C. I said and did the following: _____

_____

_____

   D. If I were to have a second chance, I would say and do the following: _____

_____

_____

_____

For most people, one of the most difficult situations to handle constructively occurs when someone is angry in our presence; worse still if they are angry at us. Our most likely response if the anger is directed at someone else is to (1) tell or ask the other person not to feel or express their anger (it's not "nice," "polite," "comfortable" for us to hear); or (2) defend the person they are angry with (especially if it is someone close to us); or (3) support their anger and tell them they should be angry. If they are angry at us, we are most likely to become defensively angry in return. All of these responses present potential problems.

As discussed in the opening chapter, emotions don't go away just because you don't want them to be experienced. Telling someone that they "shouldn't" have a feeling tends to (1) make them angry with you for not trying to understand; (2) cause them to no longer talk with you about that or other issues that bother them; or (3) make them feel guilty for having their feeling. In most cases, becoming defensively angry only inflames the situation. Suggesting to a very angry person that they "calm down and act rationally" is generally like pouring oil on fire. When you have been very angry and another person has used any of the above approaches, how did you feel?

RESPONSES TO ANGER

List several times when *you* were very angry and another person said or did something that (1) made you feel worse; (2) made you feel better.

Situation	Other's Reaction	Your Feeling and Response

The guidelines below will be helpful to you in constructively dealing with angry persons, whether their anger is directed at you or others.

1. When people are angry, assume they are in pain. Anger is usually a secondary emotion. It is preceded by disappointment, hurt, fear, etc. Anger is one way of responding to these primary feelings.

2. When people are in pain, they want recognition of their pain first. They do not want to be "rational," "calm," "mature," or any of the other things we tell them to be at that moment. (Remember how you felt when someone told you to be rational when you were angry?)

3. If you keep quiet and just listen, trying to understand where the pain is coming from, you will have better information on which to proceed and you will avoid the major danger in this situation—the defensive counterattack.

4. Do not get defensive, do not counterattack. If you counterattack, then there will be two very angry people and that will make the problem much worse.

5. Talk the angry person down. First listen and occasionally paraphrase to see if you are hearing correctly. Doing this will begin to calm the angry person. When he or she is less angry, increase your use of paraphrasing and begin to ask questions and for clarification.

6. When he or she is calmed down, then problem solve, present your side, confront, etc.

When dealing with an angry person, you need to examine your goal in the interaction. If you want to help that person to become less uncomfortable, if you want to understand why he is upset, if you want to help him to work out a resolution of what is bothering him, then you need to keep the following in mind. Consider that someone who is very angry is on a temporary "drug trip," metaphorically speaking. The "drug" is adrenalin and reacts within the person's system to cause great arousal, uncomfortable symptoms, and external signs of distress. To get that person to the point where he or she will be calm enough to listen to you, examine his or her own point of view, and search for a resolution, you will have to "talk him or her down" from the "trip." Keep in mind that perceptual distortion is greatest when someone is emotionally aroused, feels vulnerable, and is threatened. Angry people will be engaging in selective perception and perceptual distortion to a greater degree than usual. Because you may become defensive yourself, you too will begin to distort what they are saying to or about you. This is a time for paraphrasing and listening. Below is a model for dealing with angry others. For each "stage of anger" your response should vary depending on your desired goal. Obviously, the judging of what "stage of anger" the other person is in must be made subjectively by you on the spot.

STRATEGIES FOR DEALING WITH ANGER				
Anger	**Person's Need**	**Your Response**	**Don't**	**Goal**
HIGH	Recognition for their pain.	Keep quiet and listen. Brief paraphrase of their feelings, e.g., "You are more upset than I realized."	Say "Calm down" or "You're making mountains out of molehills."	Avoid making the person more angry. Stay calm.
MEDIUM	Understanding of their position.	Paraphrase the content of his or her message and apparent feelings to test the accuracy of your understanding.	Defend yourself.	Understand his or her point of view.
LOW	Resolution.	Paraphrase. Confrontation. Problem solving. Your explanation of your point of view.	Use derogatory labels. Don't try to "win" or place blame.	Resolution.

When you try this approach, you will notice that the other persons will begin to lower the intensity of their anger. As they do, you alter your response to follow them down the scale. Should they become angry again, you alter your approach to follow them back up the scale, just listening and recognizing that they seem upset again. In most cases, if you listen and try to understand rather than defend yourself, they will calm down quickly. This is most difficult to do with loved ones and with people who have a great deal of perceived power over you. In addition, although most people will respond well most of the time to this approach, a few individuals may choose to remain angry regardless of what you try. This may be due to their insecurity or extreme upset or to their desire to nurse a grudge. You can either give up at that point or confront them, e.g., "I can't help but notice that each time I try to understand your point of view you get angry all over again. Do you or don't you want to try to work this out?"

COMMON EXCUSES FOR NOT CHANGING COMMUNICATION STYLE. Four common objections, excuses really, for not improving one's communication skills are discussed below.

1. *Paraphrasing and techniques for improving communication approaches are phony, contrived, artificial, dishonest—"not me."*

You were not born with your style of communicating encoded on your genes. You learned to express your ideas and feelings verbally and nonverbally from your family members and other significant people in your life. Even if you think you are rebelling against a style you did not like during childhood, someone still provided you with a model against which to compare yourself. Since you learned your current style somewhere from someone, you can learn to alter that style if you wish. New behaviors and newly learned skills feel awkward until practiced enough so they become second nature. It takes time and work to develop new skills and break old habits.

2. *Relationships should just "happen." Planning my responses in hopes of influencing others' reactions is manipulative.*

We don't hesitate to get training and engage in extensive practice when learning new job skills or recreational activities. Relationships are probably harder to build and easier to destroy than any other aspect of our lives. They are too valuable to health and happiness to be left entirely to trial-and-error approaches. Thoughtfulness in how you handle people's feelings will increase your chances of helpful, healthful relationships. Besides, we usually want things to turn out in a way that satisfies us, and we do try to influence others to meet our needs. The term *manipulation* has a bad connotation only if the person is being taken advantage of and left unsatisfied. If you can *both* feel comfortable and still get what you want, then manipulation toward that end is beneficial. Since you try to influence others anyway, you might as well do it thoughtfully, so that both parties feel good in the interaction.

3. *If I am honest about my feelings, the situation may get worse; the other persons may be angry with me, they may tell me things about myself I don't want to hear.*

These concerns are valid. These consequences may occur. You can significantly reduce the odds that the first two will be the outcomes by following the type of communication guidelines discussed here. However, you are only part of the equation. You can only control your own behavior. Even if you phrase your approach perfectly, the other persons may still react defensively or hostilely because of their styles. Some people will not tolerate any expression of feelings and/or critical feedback. They may be insecure, angry, emotionally ill, etc.—factors having nothing to do with you. If the other person appears to be misinterpreting or distorting what you are trying to say, use paraphrasing to check out his or her perceptions. Remember, although improving your communication ability improves the chances of satisfactory exchanges, it does not guarantee it in all cases. There may be situations and persons with whom it is not wise to be too candid. You will have to develop your own sense of timing and intuition. Last, of course, the other person may share feelings and opinions about you once you've established that as a ground rule.

4. *Changing my style of communication is too much work.*

If you are telling yourself this nonsense, ask yourself, "What is in it for me to stay the way I am?"

Overview of Interpersonal Relationships

It seems paradoxical to view intimate relationships as potential stressors, especially in view of the importance of maintaining support networks. It is not the relationships themselves that are stressful but the expectations we have for the relationships. Many people are hurt, and many worthwhile relationships are terminated, because of unrealistic or unshared expectations.

Disappointment is an inevitable part of any close relationship, particularly between lovers, married or unmarried. We don't expect strangers or casual friends to go out of their way to anticipate and meet our emotional and physical needs. We do expect parents, children, very close friends, and lovers to anticipate and provide for us even without our asking. The closer we feel emotionally to people, the more we tend to expect from them in the way of support and thoughtfulness. The more we expect from them, the more things there are for them to be aware of in terms of our needs. The more they must be aware of, the greater the likelihood they will forget or overlook something, not do it according to our expectations, or not do it because of fatigue or even resentment that so much is expected of them. The closer we are emotionally to someone, the more thoughtful, sensitive, considerate, and superhuman we expect them to be. Thus we tend to think, "If she *really* loved me, she would do it for me." "If he *really* loved me, he would know without my having to ask or remind him." "If she *really* loved me, she would have remembered." "If he *really* respected me, he would never have done that." "If she *loved me,* she would express her love in the same way I express my love for her." "If he really loved me, he would not have mentioned it again." These illogical assumptions are probably the basis for a large percentage of divorces and other problems in close relationships.

People can love us (and we can love them) without being able to anticipate and satisfy all our (their) needs all the time. It may be reasonable to expect our parents, friends, and lovers to care about us, to listen and try to understand most of the time, and to share many—but not all—of our interests. But they (and we) can still feel anger, disappointment, selfishness, and resentment at times within the boundaries of a caring, loving relationship. Our relationships are likely to last much longer if we realize our friends and lovers cannot read our minds, that they have their own weaknesses, preoccupations, and insecurities, and will sometimes "let us down." We need to allow our parents, friends, and lovers to be as human as we wish they would allow us to be.

A not uncommon reaction to severe disappointment in close relationships is withdrawal from intimacy. Some individuals avoid becoming emotionally close to others for fear of rejection or betrayal or the fear of being overwhelmed by the other's needs and demands. Discomfort with taking care of others can have numerous causes. It is important to note your avoidance of emotional involvement—sharing, trusting, confiding, depending, and giving to others. Whether you fear pain or you are more comfortable taking than giving in a relationship, professional counseling can be helpful. Either reaction may seriously affect the extent and quality of your support network.

EXPECTATIONS OF RELATIONSHIPS

For each category, list the people in your life. Then list your basic expectation for the way they behave in their relationship with you. Then indicate those expectations that are probably unrealistic. List the times or events to which you responded by feeling let down, hurt, betrayed, used, etc. Check those painful experiences that may have been the result of or were contributed to by your unrealistic expectations for that person.

People	Expectations	Realistic?	Painful Experiences	Check
Family of origin (parents, children, siblings, and relatives)				
Lover(s)/Spouse				
Friends				
Others				

Decision Making

Your decision making can have a major impact on your health. Bad decisions can lead to uncomfortable situations, which in turn can result in severe or chronic stress reactions. How you make decisions also depends, in part, on the degree to which you believe you have the power to influence the outcome of a specific situation or your life in general. People who think that what happens to them is a result of fate or is caused solely by the behavior of others who cannot be influenced tend to be less thoughtful and more impulsive in reaching decisions.

Decision making involves a clear understanding of what you want, what problems are involved in reaching your goal, the options you have to try to reach that goal, and the consequences, pro and con, of each possible choice. With that information, you have the information you need to make a well-informed decision. Putting off the decision is still a decision. You cannot *not* choose. To decide not to decide *is a decision* to allow others or events to determine the outcome without any potential influence from you.

There are numerous models for decision making. Most follow the guidelines discussed above. Below is an approach that will often be helpful to you. Take a problem or decision that is pending in your life. If you choose, take a problem or decision you have already faced and rework it to see what you might have done differently.

APPROACH TO DECISION MAKING

1. State the problem or choice briefly and clearly. _____
_____

2. What is your goal? (e.g., What is it you think you want to do about the problem? What would you like to have happen after your choice?) _____
_____
_____

3. List all possible choices, options, or alternatives to bring about your goal, regardless of their practicality—be creative.

    a. _____

    b. _____

    c. _____

    d. _____

    e. _____

    f. _____

4. For each option, list the things in favor of and the things against choosing this approach.

Option	Pros	Cons
a.		
b.		

---

continued

Option	Pros	Cons
c.		
d.		
e.		
f.		

5. Choose the alternative you believe gives you the best chance of achieving your goal.

My first choice is:_____

_____

6. Now look at the persons and factors that may make it difficult to achieve your goal with this approach and those persons and factors that may be helpful.

HELPFUL PEOPLE AND FACTORS

_____
_____
_____
_____

HOW CAN YOU UTILIZE THESE HELPFUL FACTORS?

_____
_____
_____
_____
_____

RESTRICTIVE PEOPLE AND FACTORS

_____
_____
_____
_____

HOW CAN YOU MINIMIZE THE HARMFUL EFFECT OF THESE RESTRICTIVE FACTORS?

_____
_____
_____
_____

SOCIAL STRESSORS AND SUPPORTERS REVISITED

Social Stressors: *Those organizations and people to whom you relate and that are potentially stressful to you. These are the factors with which most of us are familiar. However, although we may be familiar with these factors, we are often not aware of how much stress they are producing in our lives.*

Social Supporters: *Those social factors to which you are potentially exposed and which tend to have a healing effect and which protect you from social stressors.*

In "revisiting" environmental social stressors and supporters, we do so in the context of the particular *situation* in which you find yourself. The last section, Internal Factors, showed how your personality may interact with the situational factors you face to increase your stress. However, there are objective situational factors that *contribute* to the stress you experience, irrespective of your attitudes, communication skills, and so on. For example, some people's style creates stress even when the situation itself is relatively pressure-free. There are also common situational factors, particularly the nature of the task(s) and role(s) you are expected to perform, that add to or act as primary stressors.

The Interpersonal Factor

If you are experiencing problems in your relationships with people who are important in your life, you are likely to experience tension. You may be the *major cause* of the problem; you may be one of the *contributing factors* (with no one person to "blame"); or you may be a relatively *innocent bystander*. Everyone else in your life, on the job and at home, suffers from the same type of stress-related tendencies. When colleagues or family members are not handling their own stress well, they may be acting in a way that produces stress for you. They may become angry, irritable, blaming, or inefficient, thus leaving you with more than your share of work or social responsibility. They may become withdrawn or may dramatically change their behavior. They may become depressed or anxious. Changes in behavior—such as sleep patterns, moodiness, eating habits (see Chapter 1)—may indicate stress.

Rather than responding as though the whole thing were your fault (by becoming angry, defensive, hurt, etc.), try to talk with the other person about your observations, use paraphrasing, and see (1) if he or she is having difficulty coping with pressure; and (2) to what extent, if any, you are contributing to the problem. Next, talk about how you might be helpful to him or her. Good communication skills are often critical in this type of situation. If you believe you need to learn more about handling this type of situation constructively, then get some additional education in this area.

Task-Based Stress

On the job and in our personal life, there are often tasks which we take on voluntarily, tasks which are assigned to us, and tasks which

---

SOCIAL STRESSORS

Excessive responsibility for making major decisions

No or ambiguous standards by which to judge one's performance

Lack of time or facilities to perform one's responsibilities adequately

Unclear or conflicting expectations of your responsibilities

Inadequate praise and recognition from others

Conflict with significant persons in your life

Inadequate support network

SOCIAL SUPPORTERS

Appropriate responsibility

Clear standards and expectations by which others judge your performance

Adequate time and opportunity to perform one's responsibilities

Adequate time between major life changes and events

Adequate support network

Adequate praise and recognition from others

Minimal conflict with significant persons in your life

automatically come with our role. Stress is a likely result if you score high on the following scale.

SCALE 14–SOCIAL STRESSORS: TASK-BASED STRESS

Score each from 5 to 1 depending on the extent that the statements made are true for you.*

5	4	3	2	1
Always	**Often**	**Sometimes**	**Rarely**	**Never**

ON THE JOB	OFF THE JOB	
_____	_____	**1.** I am personally responsible for making decisions that have significant consequences. Comment: _____
_____	_____	**2.** The difficulty of performing the task may exceed my realistic ability to perform it to the desired specifications, but I can't or don't want to get out of the responsibility Comment: _____
_____	_____	**3.** The requirements and standards by which my performance is to be judged are ambiguous: I'm either not sure exactly what is to be done or how I am to be judged. Comment: _____
_____	_____	**4.** What I need to do is clear, but there is so much to do that I can't meet all the demands on time. Comment: _____
_____	_____	**5.** There is so much that needs to be done that I can't do it all; there is no clear way to make a priority list to reduce the overload. Comment: _____
_____	_____	Totals

This also applies to those who have primary responsibility for running the home and caring for the family.

REMEDIES: Task-based stress may be helped by a variety of approaches depending on the nature of the pressure:

1. Education and training enhance abilities that make the performance of the task easier and more efficient, for example, training in time management.

2. Gaining more information about tasks and expected standards may reduce pressure.

3. Putting the task load in priority lists is helpful, with realistic time goals for each task.

4. Delegating responsibility relieves pressure.

5. Evaluating your managerial style or your style of reacting to pressure and making appropriate changes gives you more flexibility to adapt to altering situations.

6. Seeking organizational or management consultants may help identify stress and reduce employee inefficiency.

7. In your personal life, develop the ability to discuss your pressures and interpersonal strains with friends and relatives. Try to negotiate the differences in expectations that are helping to create stress between you. If you are not able to do this alone, professional counselors and/or training courses in communications skills will be helpful.

Role-Based Stress

We sometimes experience stress due to our roles. You should be aware of the following:

1. Roles are sets of expectations for our behavior that we and others impose on ourselves that may be independent of work performance standards.

2. The role tells us *how* to behave according to socially agreed upon standards. For example, in traditional families of origin, mothers were often expected to be martyrs. Fathers were expected to work long hours away from the family and were not accountable for their time. Children were to be seen and not heard. Women were to be docile, and men assertive.

3. We play multiple roles in our daily lives. At home we are spouses, parents, friends, and relatives; at work, we may have a number of titles.

4. We cannot escape roles, but we can recognize which ones we play and how they affect our health and behavior.

SCALE 15–SOCIAL STRESSORS: ROLE-BASED STRESS

Check the following according to the degree to which you feel each may be a problem area for you. Mark your answers in the appropriate column.

5	4	3	2	1
No Problem	**Slight Problem**	**Moderate Problem**	**Serious Problem**	**Very Serious Problem**

AT WORK	AT HOME			
_____	_____	1. At work, colleagues seem to expect things from me that are different from what I think I am supposed to be doing. Comment: _____ _____		

continued

5	4	3	2	1
No Problem	**Slight Problem**	**Moderate Problem**	**Serious Problem**	**Very Serious Problem**

AT WORK	AT HOME	
————	————	**2.** At work, what I expect from my colleagues does not always seem to be what they think their jobs entail. Comments or examples: _____ _____
————	————	**3.** At home, members of my family seem unhappy about my work schedule. Comments or examples: _____ _____
————	————	**4.** At home, family members seem to want things from me that are different from what I think I should be doing or that I am comfortable doing. Comments or examples: _____ _____
————	————	**5.** Try as I might, I don't seem to be able to keep everyone at work and at home pleased at the same time. Comments or examples: _____ _____
————	————	**6.** At work, it is not always clear to me what is expected of me in order to perform well. The criteria sometimes seem vague or shifting. Comments or examples: _____ _____
————	————	**7.** At home, it is not always clear what my family members want or expect of me. Comments or examples: _____ _____
————	———— Totals	

The following exercise is designed to help you to examine your changing responsibilities.

CHANGING RESPONSIBILITIES

1. List responsibilities given up within the past year. _____

_____

_____

2. List responsibilities currently carried. _____

_____

continued

---

3. List new responsibilities taken on recently. _____

_____

_____

4. List responsibilities you anticipate assuming within the next year._____

_____

_____

ROLE PROBLEMS. What you expect of yourself and what others expect from you may be very clear, but the expectations may at times be mutually exclusive, thus leading to *role conflict:* the inability to perform all your roles adequately, when expected, because they conflict. For example, as a *woman,* some may expect you to be nonassertive, but as a *supervisor* or *executive,* you are expected to be firm and direct. Therefore, as a *woman executive,* you may experience *role conflict.* What you are expected to do, by yourself or by others, may not be clearly articulated, at least to you, thus leading to *role ambiguity.* For example, you are promoted and given a new title but no clear idea of *how* you are supposed to act. Many new supervisors act in an authoritarian manner on assuming the position because they think that is how they are *expected* to manage people. Usually a more flexible "consultant/teacher" model is more appropriate and may be expected by management although not so stated explicitly. And what about those ambiguous roles of *parent* or *spouse?* Many marital and parent/ child relationships flounder and die because neither party ever realizes that their mutual tension stems from different expectations about *how* the *other* is to behave. What you are expected to do, by yourself and others, may be clear and may not conflict, but there may be so much that you can't do it all, thus leading to *role strain.* For example, can you be a *mother, employee, spouse, parent, daughter-in-law, friend* to different people, *scout leader,* and *school board member*—and still have time for *yourself* to everyone's satisfaction?

ROLE PROBLEMS		
Indicate your personal experience with the following concepts both on the job and in your personal life.		
	On the Job	**In Your Personal Life**
Role Conflict		
Role Ambiguity		

continued

	On the Job	In Your Personal Life
Role Strain		

REMEDIES. Problems with roles result when people do not think about (or care about) the expectations they place on each other at work or at home. Identifying the roles being played and the possible areas of conflict can lead to renegotiating these roles in order to relieve stress.

1. Seek clarification within your work or family about the roles others expect you to play and the roles you think they are supposed to be playing. Ask the people around you the following questions:
   a. What would you like me to do *more often* in order to help you do your job better?
   b. What would you like me to do *less often* in order for you to get your job done more efficiently?
   c. What am I doing that is *just right* as far as you are concerned?
   d. Are you willing to negotiate these requests with me? (A written agreement with a specific date on which you meet to assess your progress is very helpful.) (See also Problem Solving Exercise, page 86.)

2. Make certain that everybody has the same understanding about these expectations.

3. Realize that there is no way you will be able to please everybody all the time. Some roles will take second place no matter what you decide.

4. Talk with others about what you think they expect of you, what you expect of yourself.

5. If your roles are putting too much stress on you, be willing to change some of the rules under which you operate.

6. Organize time for various roles (e.g., family, job). Learn to manage your time.

7. At the work place, if these suggestions do not seem to work for you, (1) your perceptions may be distorted; recheck the section on attitudes and talk with trusted people who will be *honest* with you; and (2) your organization might profit from the assistance of a management consultant who could teach personnel how to identify and negotiate role conflicts.

8. If there are role-related problems in your marriage or family that you cannot resolve, professional counselors can help.

Distribution of Resources and Interests

As the extent and variety of your support network relate to longevity and quality of health, so do the number and quality of your activities. People who have a limited number of interests run the risk of ending up with all their eggs in one or two baskets. Recognition of this fact breeds anxiety and sometimes desperate efforts to ward off change to protect those fragile baskets. Should events or illness or handicap or age curtail the ability to perform those few special activities, the individual can suffer severe, even fatal stress. For example, the woman who devotes her entire life, her self-image, and all her training to being a home manager, wife, and mother risks depression and anxiety when her children leave home and/or her spouse dies or divorces her. The individual, who devotes his or her life's effort to work can suffer depression or anxiety upon retirement. A person whose self-esteem is based on perceived sexual appeal can feel that life is over when he or she loses the attractiveness, grows older, or suffers some type of disfigurement.

It is important to distribute your eggs in a variety of baskets. This means liking and respecting yourself for a number of different reasons and not just one or two. For example, "I am a great athlete. People know and admire me as a hero because of my athletic achievements. But, what will I do to earn that respect when I can't perform up to par as I age?" Many professional athletes have felt the best years of their lives over while in their thirties because of retirement. Feeling they have nothing else at which they excel leads them to depression and a life devoted to dreaming about the past. It is important to have hobbies and recreational activities—both active and passive, intellectual and physical. It is important to have several friends who can meet different needs and to try and develop talents in more than one area for your personal entertainment.

It is important to learn to please yourself even if others don't applaud your efforts, as well as to learn to enjoy the journey itself rather than holding back your excitement until you reach the end. The end is the end. It is the trip and whatever you can find along the way that provide the rewards.

EGGS IN YOUR BASKETS
List below the people in your life whom you enjoy being with and the events and activities that give you pleasure or satisfaction. Both your friends and your preferred activities should add to your sense of well-being. How many baskets do you have?

Additional Situational Factors Related to Stress

Adams and associates have summarized the situational factors related to stress as *recent* and *ongoing events on* and *off* the job. Research in 1977 by Adams found that the more adjustments a manager had to make on the job, the more likely he would experience chronic health problems. When these types of stressors occur to large numbers of people *already working under stressful conditions* (see pages 108–109), the incidence of sick leave, accidents, and poor attention to work rises significantly. Examine the examples below and check those that apply to you.

SCALE 16–SOCIAL STRESS: SITUATIONAL FACTORS

Recent Events on the Job

_____   **1.** Major changes in instructions, policies, or procedures.

List:_____

_____

_____   **2.** Requirement to work more hours per week than normal.

Comment: _____

_____

_____   **3.** Sudden significant increase in activity level or pace of work.

Comment: _____

_____

_____   **4.** Major reorganization.

Comment: _____

_____

_____   **5.** Can you identify other changes that have occurred on your job?

_____ _____

_____ _____

_____ _____

_____ _____

Recent Events off the Job

_____   **1.** Restriction of social life

List:_____

_____

_____   **2.** Marriage

Comment: _____

_____

_____   **3.** Serious illness

List:_____

_____

——————— **4.** Traumatic disruption of a close relationship

List:_____

_____

——————— **5.** Loss of status or self-esteem, a defeat, or humiliation

Comment: _____

_____

——————— **6.** The anniversary date of a traumatic disruption of a close relationship. (Many people experience strong emotions around these times, even years afterward.)

List dates of deaths, separations, sad occurrences, going back *at least* 10 years.

Incident	**Date**

——————— **7.** Loss of valued possessions

List:_____

_____

_____

——————— **8.** A triumph, public recognition, a reunion, etc.

List:_____

_____

_____

——————— **9.** Others (specify) _____

_____

_____

_____

These ongoing job conditions have been categorized by researchers under the headings of *work overload, role ambiguity, role conflict, territoriality, poor interpersonal relations,* and *lack of participation.* Research has shown that managers experiencing these problems display *chronic health problems* and feel ineffective and dissatisfied on their jobs. This probably is true also for home managers.

Check the following daily work conditions that have
been shown to be very stressful as they apply to you.

_____   **1.** Work overload

                  Comment: _____

                  _____

_____   **2.** Feedback only on unsatisfactory performance

                  Comment: _____

                  _____

_____   **3.** Lack of confidence in management

                  Comment: _____

                  _____

_____   **4.** Role ambiguity

                  List: _____

                  _____

_____   **5.** Role conflict

                  List: _____

                  _____

_____   **6.** Unresolved interpersonal conflict

                  List: _____

                  _____

_____   **7.** "Fire-fighting" style of problem solving by management rather than working
                  from a plan

                  Comment: _____

                  _____

_____   **8.** Interunit conflict

                  List: _____

                  _____

_____   **9.** Others

                  _____

                  _____

                  _____

These types of ongoing work stressors come about because of the habits, expectations, and styles of the people involved, particularly the managers. Changing these factors is not a matter that can be rectified by executive order. Change requires altering the behavior of all personnel, particularly members of management. Changing group norms may necessitate the use of a management consultant skilled in team building who will teach each work unit to increase efficiency and reduce conflict by eliminating stumbling blocks to productivity and by improving interpersonal communication.

If your work includes household management and these conditions apply to you, you and your spouse are the "work teams" that may require assistance. Children and other adults living with you or affecting the family need also to be considered part of the problem and the potential solution.

LIFE STAGES. We all pass through similar life stages* that encompass pivotal events, or milestones, common to our culture.

Individuals react so variously to these events that it is difficult to give any hard and fast predictions about how you will respond to them. It is sufficient that you recognize these events and the transition from one life stage to another as being potentially stressful and that you make the effort to function creatively in the face of inevitable change.

*These have been commonly designated as: late teens through twenties; thirties through mid-forties; and mid-forties through sixty and beyond. If you are unsuccessful in solving the transition problems on your own, talk to an appropriate friend or professional.

LIFE STAGE STRESSORS

Acquiring an education

Marriage

Leaving parents' home

Establishing a home of one's own

Starting a family

Becoming established in a profession

Menopause

Children leaving home

Promotions

Retirement

Disability/death of a spouse

Unemployment

Fulfillment or abandonment of one's youthful aspirations

LIFE STAGE EXERCISE

For each of the broad categories below, indicate the major issues for you whether past, current, or anticipated.

Age Range	Issues and Stressors for You
17–30	
30–45	
45–60	
60+	

RECENT EVENTS AS STRESSORS. Research indicates that changes in your health are directly related to the number of changes you experience in a given period of your life. High life-change scores on the Holmes-Rahe scale are correlated with a wide variety of health changes from mental disorders to injuries to serious illness. In general, the higher your score, the greater risk you run of experiencing a serious health problem of some sort. Doctor Rahe's research included studies of 2500 naval personnel. He discovered that 30 percent of the individuals with the highest scores on the life-change scale experienced almost 90 percent more illness during the initial month of a cruise than did the 30 percent with the lowest scores. The high-change-score group consistently experienced more illness than did the low-scoring group.

When you fill out the Social Readjustment Scale, remember that your score is not an *absolute* indicator of what will happen to you. It only indicates the degree of risk you face compared to a large sample of others with similar scores. These statistics can predict the *percentage* of a group of people who will become ill, but cannot predict which *individuals* in the group will experience illness. Individuals who are aware of the stress factors in their lives and understand how to reduce or tolerate stress have a better chance of maintaining their health even with a high life-change score.

The closer in time that the change has occurred, the greater the impact on your health, in general. The effect on your health of your score today is likely to influence you from 6 to 24 months. Rate your life changes over the past one to two years.

If your score is high, *do not panic*. You can influence your resistance to stress-induced problems by increasing your stress tolerance, minimizing new changes in the future, reducing additional risks to your health, and thinking twice before making any new major decisions. Read the section in this book on Increasing Stress Tolerance (page 123).

Scoring Guidelines:

−150 = one chance in three of a major health problem in the next two years.

150–300 = 50/50 chance of a major health problem in the next two years.

300+ = 90 percent chance of a major health problem in the next two years.

THE SOCIAL READJUSTMENT RATING SCALE

Life Event	Mean Value
1. Death of spouse*	100
2. Divorce	73
3. Marital separation	65
4. Detention in jail or other institution	63
5. Death of a close family member	63

*Although not included in the original research, the death of a child may be at least as, if not more, traumatic than, the death of a spouse.

Life Event	Mean Value
6. Major personal injury or illness	53
7. Marriage	50
8. Being fired at work	47
9. Marital reconciliation	45
10. Retirement from work	45
11. Major change in the health or behavior of a family member	44
12. Pregnancy	40
13. Sexual difficulties	39
14. Gaining a new family member (e.g., through birth, adoption, oldster moving in, etc.)	39
15. Major business readjustment (e.g., merger, reorganization, bankruptcy, etc.)	39
16. Major change in financial state (e.g., a lot worse off or a lot better off than usual)	38
17. Death of a close friend	37
18. Changing to a different line of work	36
19. Major change in the number of arguments with spouse (e.g., either a lot more or a lot less than usual regarding child rearing, personal habits, etc.)	35
20. Taking on a mortgage greater than $10,000 (e.g., purchasing a home, business, etc.)†	31
21. Foreclosure on a mortgage or loan	30
22. Major change in responsibilities at work (e.g., promotion, demotion, lateral transfer)	29
23. Son or daughter leaving home (e.g., marriage, attending college, etc.)	29
24. In-law troubles	29
25. Outstanding personal achievement	28
26. Wife beginning or ceasing work outside the home	26
27. Beginning or ceasing formal schooling	26
28. Major change in living conditions (e.g., building a new home, remodeling, deterioration of home or neighborhood)	25
29. Revision of personal habits (dress, manners, associations, etc.)	24
30. Troubles with the boss	23
31. Major change in working hours or conditions	20
32. Change in residence	20
33. Change to a new school	20
34. Major change in usual type and/or amount of recreation	19
35. Major change in church activities (e.g., a lot more or a lot less than usual)	19
36. Major change in social activities (e.g., clubs, dancing, movies, visiting, etc.)	18
37. Taking on a mortgage or loan of less than $10,000 (e.g., purchasing a car, TV, freezer, etc.)†	17
38. Major change in sleeping habits (a lot more or a lot less sleep, or change in part of day when asleep)	16
39. Major change in number of family get-togethers (e.g., a lot more or a lot less than usual)	15
40. Major change in eating habits (a lot more or a lot less food intake, or very different meal hours or surroundings)	15
41. Vacation	13
42. Christmas	12
43. Minor violations of the law (e.g., traffic tickets, jaywalking, disturbing the peace, etc.)	11

†Original scale does not take account of inflationary changes in our economy. Make your own definition of "large" or "small" loan or mortgage.
[From T. H. Holmes and R. H. Rahe: "The Social Readjustment Rating Scale." Journal of Psychosomatic Research 11:213–218, 1967. Reprinted with permission of Pergamon Press, Inc.]

OTHER BIOLOGICAL FACTORS RELATED TO STRESS

Genetic Stressors

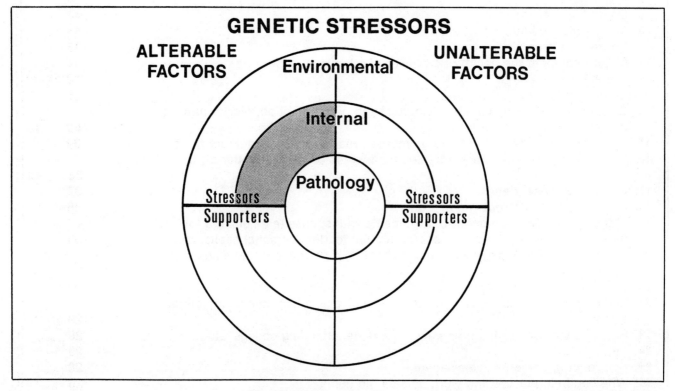

Genetic Stressors: *Those internal stressors which you inherit from ancestors and which increase your susceptibility to certain diseases with their attendant dysfunction or disability.*

The complete list of genetic stressors is too extensive to include. However, a partial list of the types of diseases that may have a hereditary component in their origin is given.

PARTIAL LIST OF GENETIC STRESSORS

Heart disease	Kidney disease
Cancer	Diseases of the large intestine
Strokes	Allergies
Diabetes	Arthritis (including gout)
Heart attacks at an early age	Skin diseases
High blood pressure	Bleeding disorders (e.g., hemophilia)
Thyroid disorders	Diseases of bones
Liver disease	Diseases of the nervous system
Alcoholism	Psychiatric disorders
Lung disease	Any other known hereditary disorder
Congenital defects	Other
Obesity (overweight)	

SCALE 17–GENETIC STRESSORS

In order to determine your family medical history, please fill out the following questionnaire, checking each column with regard to whether you or anyone in your family (father, mother, brothers, sisters, aunts, uncles, cousins who are blood-related) suffered from the conditions listed.

No	Yes	Don't Know	
————	————	————	**1.** Heart disease
			Comment:_____
————	————	————	**2.** Cancer
			Comment:_____
————	————	————	**3.** Strokes
			Comment:_____
————	————	————	**4.** Diabetes
			Comment:_____
————	————	————	**5.** Heart attacks at an early age
			Comment:_____
————	————	————	**6.** Thyroid disorder
			Comment:_____
————	————	————	**7.** Liver disease
			Comment:_____
————	————	————	**8.** Alcoholism
			Comment:_____
————	————	————	**9.** Lung disease
			Comment:_____
————	————	————	**10.** Any congenital (birth) defects
			Comment:_____
————	————	————	**11.** Obesity (overweight)
			Comment:_____

continued

No	Yes	Don't Know	
———	———	———	**12.** Kidney disease
			Comment:_____
———	———	———	**13.** Disease of the large intestine
			Comment:_____
———	———	———	**14.** Allergies
			Comment:_____
———	———	———	**15.** Arthritis (including gout)
			Comment:_____
———	———	———	**16.** Skin disease
			Comment:_____
———	———	———	**17.** Bleeding disorders (e.g., hemophilia)
			Comment:_____
———	———	———	**18.** Any known hereditary disorders
			Comment:_____
———	———	———	**19.** Disease of the bones
			Comment:_____
———	———	———	**20.** Disease of the nervous system
			Comment:_____
———	———	———	**21.** Other (please list)

continued

If your answer to any of these questions is yes, then please list on the chart below the family members with the disorder.			
Name	**Present Age or Age at Death**	**Sex**	**Disorder or Disease**

If you do not know the answers to the questions, then you should do your best to find out the answers from your surviving relatives. Remember to list only blood relatives. Relatives by marriage do not transmit their genes to you.

You may have little or nothing written on the above chart, in which case these factors may be totally insignificant. However, no matter what you have written, you should bring the list in to your family doctor the next time you have a physical. At that time, you should ask him to review it with you and ask him to help you determine the significance of your findings. Many of these problems require further evaluation to determine their significance.

Genetic Supporters

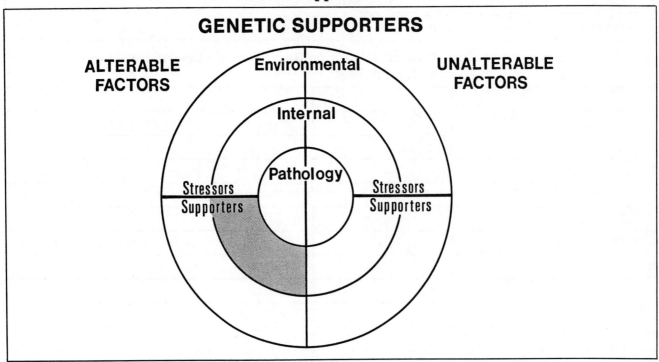

Genetic Supporters: *Those internal supporters that are inherited and have a tendency to promote your health and well-being.*

These factors are not very well defined. However, if in your family there is a tendency for people to be healthy and long-lived, then that is more likely to happen to you. You should be aware, however, that a healthy family does not guarantee your health. You must still adopt a sensible life-style in order to maximize your chances for health.

Immunity

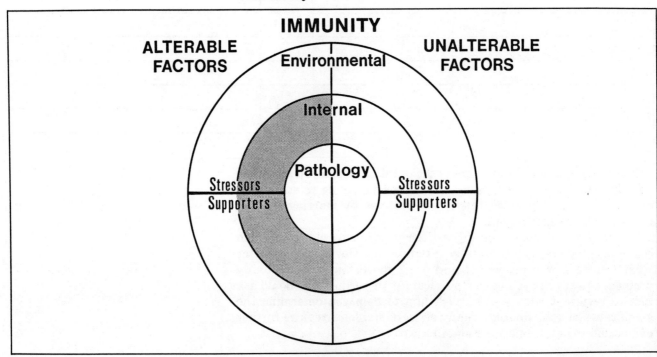

Immunity: *The body's resistance to abnormal conditions, especially those resulting from germs (infectious diseases).*

The immune response is one way in which you respond to certain environmental stressors. Your present immune status determines the way in which your immune system will respond to the presence of certain environmental chemicals and organisms which contact the skin or enter your body. A properly functioning immune system allows the individual to function normally and to survive in an environment that contains many potentially lethal organisms. Certain immune re-actions do have rare side effects which are detrimental. These may range from a mild allergic response (e.g., hay fever) to the severe, even fatal, allergic reaction (e.g., bee-sting anaphylaxis). In these cases, and others, survival is sometimes jeopardized by a system in the body that is designed to promote survival.

An individual's immune status is determined by a complex of intern-al variables that are constantly changing. Nutritional status, prior exposure to biological stressors, prior experience with certain non-biological chemicals, the immune "memory" system, internal hor-mones, immunizations, and attitude are just a few of the factors which are known to affect the functioning of the immune system.

Immunological Stressors

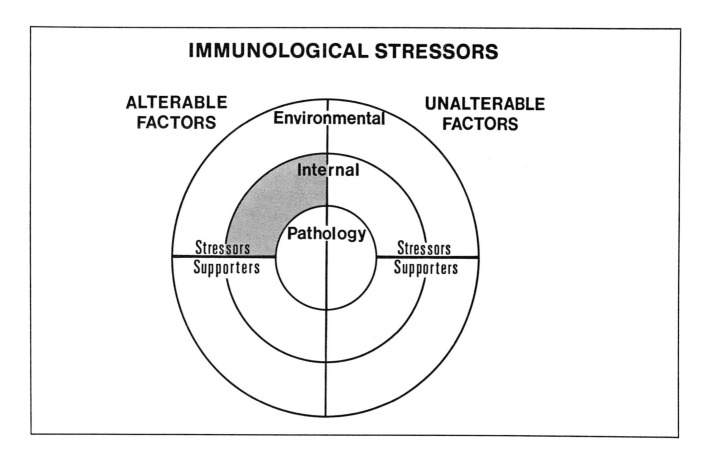

Immunological Stressors: *Those internal stressors which result from inappropriate immune responses, that is, immune responses that either fail to be protective or tend to be self-destructive.*

Immunological stressors are defined as those internal stressors that result from immune reactions. There are certain immune reactions in which the individual appears to have an inappropriate response in that the end result of the response tends to be self-destructive: for example, in severe allergic reactions to bee stings. Other allergic reactions to chemical and biological stressors, (e.g., pollen, poison ivy), are environmental agents that may induce immunological stress. Many other biological and chemical agents may induce stress through the immune system (see Biological and Chemical Stressors, Chapter 2). These allergic reactions are poorly understood medical phenomena that are too complex for detailed discussion here.

Immunological Supporters

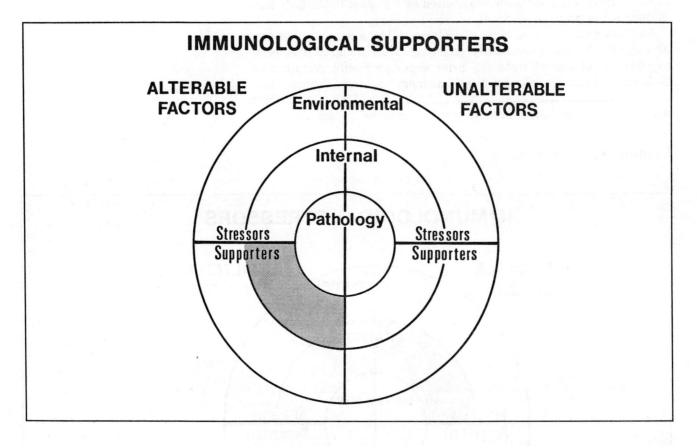

Immunological Supporters: *Those internal supporters which result from the proper functioning of the immune system and tend to be protective or self-healing.*

Immunological supporters may be defined as those internal supporters that result from immune reactions. The immune system is an important mechanism whereby we can function in an environment loaded with potential invading microorganisms, such as viruses and bacteria. This system maintains the inside of the body virtually germ-free, or at least in balance with our environmental "friends." We have the obligation to make sure we are fully immunized in order to take advantage of the protection our immune system can provide for us. Please examine the following chart in order to make sure you are fully immunized.

The following immunization schedules are generally recommended for protection against certain infectious diseases. Check that you and your children's immunizations are up to date. Your family doctor can help you determine what is maximum immunization protection for your family and what additional immunizations might be advisable. In some cases, a physician might alter the standard immunization schedule if he thinks it is necessary. Under certain circumstances, as in travel abroad and exposure to certain infectious diseases such as hepatitis, additional immunizations may be needed. Some individuals with certain chronic diseases may require special immunizations; for example, some people with chronic lung diseases will need pneumococcal vaccine to protect them from some bacterial strains that can cause pneumonia.

IMMUNIZATION CHART*						
Oral Polio	DPT	TD	MMR	Mumps	Measles	Rubella
Polio	[Diphtheria, Pertussis, Tetanus]	[Tetanus, Diphtheria]	[Measles, Mumps, Rubella]	[Mumps]	[Measles]	[German Measles]
2 months 4 months 6 months 18 months 5 years or two doses 8 weeks apart; a 3rd dose 8–12 months later; and 4th dose at 5 years of age. Given to adults under special circumstances.	2 months 4 months 6 months 18 months 5 years or three doses 8 weeks apart with booster at 5 years of age. Not to be given above 6 years of age.	Above 6 years of age in place of DPT; three doses 8 weeks apart. Adults every 10 years.	Twelve to 15 months or 4 weeks after DPT and oral polio if over 1 year old. Can be given separately or in combination; if given separately, 6–8 weeks apart.	Often given to susceptible adults. Susceptibility can be determined by a blood test.	Advised for susceptible children and adults; that is, those previously immunized at less than 12 months or prior to 1969 or who never have had measles.	Advised for children and women of childbearing age who are susceptible. Susceptibility can be determined by a test.

*When given, the vaccine (column head) protects against the disease(s) (in brackets).

Having reviewed the Immunization Chart, please complete the following scale.

SCALE 18–IMMUNIZATION

Please list your immunization deficiencies. Place a check mark next to those immunizations for which you are delinquent.

_____ Diphtheria

_____ Tetanus

_____ Measles

_____ Mumps

_____ Rubella

_____ Pneumococcal vaccine

_____ Influenza vaccine

_____ Polio vaccine

Special Normal Internal Conditions

PREGNANCY. Probably the most stressful nonpathological human condition is pregnancy. While its primary effects are the result of changes to accommodate the growing fetus, the side effects of those changes are very stressful and sometimes debilitating. The major demands are on the mother, and they result in increased nutritional requirements and reduced exercise tolerance, as well as other changes. While many pregnant women have no problems, the side effects and complications of pregnancy often result in significant difficulties for some mothers. These often spill over into the family, resulting in major disruption because of the increased demands put on other family members.

Adjustment to the idea and fact of parenthood is often difficult. Pregnancy forces new roles and responsibilities on both men and women. For example, they may be anxious about their adequacy as parents or a woman may be concerned about her sexual attractiveness during a pregnancy and may fear a loss of control in a situation where her body and her labor now seem to dictate the course of events more than she does.

In summary, pregnancy produces many physical and emotional changes that are going to affect the mother and the entire family. While many mothers and families are able to cope easily with pregnancy and the new child, help is often welcome and useful. For those who are considering pregnancy, there are many references available. It is suggested that you pursue some of this additional reading, especially if you have not previously been pregnant or if you have had difficulty with a prior pregnancy or childbirth experience. Your physician's advice is essential in this matter.*

LACTATION (BREAST FEEDING). Like pregnancy, lactation puts extreme nutritional demands on the mother. Dietary requirements are

---

*All drugs, including alcohol and tobacco, should be avoided during pregnancy. This should begin at the time when a decision is made to have a baby because the first twelve weeks are the time when the fetus is most vulnerable. Please seek more information (e.g., "Mothering Your Unborn Baby") if you are planning a pregnancy.

dramatically increased and demands on the mother are high. Again, this can be a pleasurable and rewarding experience for a mother. Many books are available on this subject. We suggest that you consult the bibliography and your physician for help in making a choice of reading material.

MENSTRUATION. The occurrence of normal menses is a condition that increases the iron requirements for women of child-bearing age. There are other changes which accompany the menstrual cycle. Again, many women have no difficulty as a result of these normal changes. However, if this is not the case for you, check with your physician for specific advice as to what you might be able to do to improve your situation.

MENOPAUSE. The cessation of menses is a clear sign of the termination of the child-bearing years. This is a result of major hormonal changes associated with reduced ovarian function. The changes of menopause can result in many symptoms and may predispose to certain more serious (pathological) consequences. This topic should be discussed with your physician when you approach approximately 40 years of age. Many references are available. See especially, Boston Women's Heath Collective (1976).

Pathological Internal Conditions

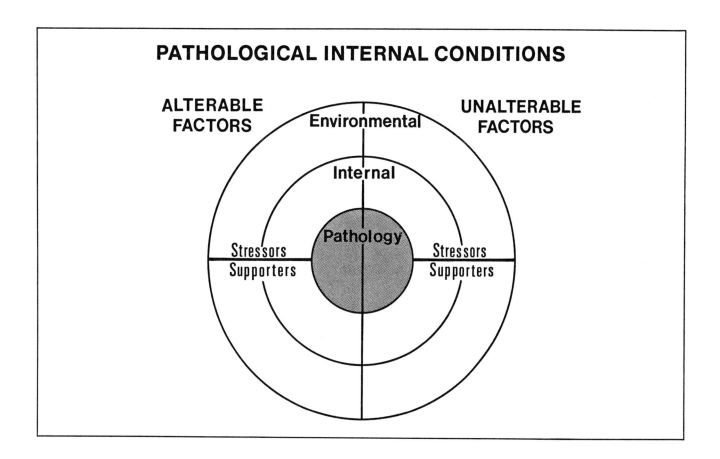

Pathology: *The last internal biological factor to be discussed, pathology, may be defined as any abnormal condition, structure, or function that results from a disease or disease process in man.*

LEVEL OF PATHOLOGY QUESTIONNAIRE

In order to define your level of pathology and its effect on your life, please fill out the following questionnaire.			Please write in the number that corresponds to the correct answer.		
5	4	3	2	1	X
Strongly Agree	**Agree**	**Neutral**	**Disagree**	**Strongly Disagree**	**Don't Know**

_____ **1.** In general, I consider myself a sickly person.

Comment: _____

_____ **2.** I feel as if I have control over nothing in my life.

Comment: _____

_____ **3.** I am very unhappy with my life circumstances in general.

Comment: _____

_____ **4.** I feel bad most of the time.

Comment: _____

_____ **5.** I am never happy.

Comment: _____

Fill in the correct answer.

6. In the past year, I have seen a health professional _____ times.

7. In the past year, I have been hospitalized for a total of _____ days.

8. I take _____ prescription medicines (number of prescriptions).

9. In the past year, I have been through _____ sets of diagnostic tests (number).

10. In the past year, I have had _____ radiation treatments (number).

11. In the past year, I have had _____ chemotherapy treatments (number).

12. In the past year, I have had _____ surgical procedures (number).

continued

5	4	3	2	1	X
Strongly Agree	**Agree**	**Neutral**	**Disagree**	**Strongly Disagree**	**Don't Know**

13. Please list the names of current diseases you have and the medicines you take.

Diseases	**Medicines**
_____	_____
_____	_____
_____	_____
_____	_____
_____	_____
_____	_____
_____	_____
_____	_____

14. Number of days lost from work in the past year because of illness: _____

15. Number of days spent in bed in the past year because of illness: _____

16. List disabilities (all chronic problems which you have that reduce your ability to function, e.g., visual loss, hearing loss, missing digits or extremities, etc.):

_____	_____
_____	_____
_____	_____
_____	_____
_____	_____
_____	_____
_____	_____

17. Which disabilities have been treated effectively (corrected to normal)? Circle those corrected to normal and mark with "T" if treated.

It is the responsibility of your personal physician to guide you through the proper management of your pathology. You are strongly encouraged to work out a program of management together that will allow you to function as independently as possible given your particular condition.

4
Increasing Stress Tolerance
Methods of Conditioning

In this chapter, you will learn to increase your tolerance to stress. Before reading this material, fill out the information below. In Chapter 5, you will be asked to review what you have written on the pretest and to devise improved methods for reacting to real-life situations such as you have described here.

IMPROVING STRESS MANAGEMENT STRATEGIES: PRE-TEST

Briefly describe two stressful situations that you have experienced recently. Indicate how you felt when you were in these situations; for example, angry, frustrated, confused, afraid, anxious, hurt, or rejected. Also discuss what you did to cope with these situations, that is, what you did to reduce the stress.

Situation 1 _____
_____
_____

How did I feel? _____
_____

How did I cope? (Specifically, what did I do mentally and behaviorally?) _____
_____
_____
_____

Situation 2 _____
_____
_____

How did I feel? _____
_____

How did I cope? (Specifically, what did I do mentally and behaviorally?) _____
_____
_____
_____

Stress tolerance may be defined as the individual's ability to withstand the cumulative effect of the stressors to which he is exposed. Stress tolerance may be changed through two basic processes: *conditioning* and *relaxation*. Both processes are active; that is, they require a decision to participate and follow through by the individual involved. *Conditioning* consists of exercise and other forms of motion (for example, dance), diet, immunization, hygiene, and risk reduction. There are many possible forms of *relaxation,* including meditation, deep-muscle relaxation, self-hypnosis, yoga, biofeedback, exercise, vacations, recreation, hobbies, music, and others.

Tranquilizers and other drugs are not recommended for general use as a means of increasing stress tolerance. They are rarely indicated and are usually not necessary. This determination must be made in conjunction with your physician.

EXERCISE AND MOTION

CONDITIONING QUESTIONNAIRE					
In order to assess your present conditioning behavior, please fill out the following questionnaire. Indicate your present utilization of the following conditioning			methods. When in doubt, please pick the higher number.		
5	4	3	2	1	X
Never	**Rarely**	**Sometimes**	**Usually**	**Always**	**Unknown**

1. I recognize the value of exercise and make an effort to incorporate it into my daily schedule.

Comment: _____

2. I exercise at least three times weekly.

Comment: _____

3. I am careful to warm up for at least five minutes prior to my vigorous exercise sessions.

Comment: _____

4. I do stretching exercises prior to and after each exercise session.

Comment: _____

5. My exercise sessions are a minimum of 20 minutes, excluding warm-up and cool-down time.

Comment: _____

6. I cool down for a minimum of five minutes after each exercise session.

Comment: _____

continued

5	4	3	2	1	X
Never	**Rarely**	**Sometimes**	**Usually**	**Always**	**Unknown**

—————— **7.** I have many alternative exercise methods; this allows me to have a flexible exercise schedule.

Comment: _____

_____

—————— **8.** My family is supportive of my efforts to do regular exercise.

Comment: _____

_____

—————— **9.** When I have taken a "vacation" from exercise, I am careful to resume and/or increase my exercise intensity gradually.

Comment: _____

_____

—————— **10.** When I sit down to a meal or am reading a menu, I am able to determine the approximate food value of the various choices, that is, the protein, fat, carbohydrate, and vitamin content.

Comment: _____

_____

—————— **11.** I am able to determine the presence or absence of food additives by reading the labels on the foods that I purchase.

Comment: _____

_____

—————— **12.** I only eat and drink foods that I am sure of in terms of purity and absence of chemicals and additives.

Comment: _____

_____

—————— **13.** I discard or return foods that appear to be spoiled or even suspicious for any reason such as appearance, smell, or taste.

Comment: _____

Answer Yes, No, or Unknown.
(1) (2)   (3)

—————— **14.** I have reviewed my immunization status with my physician, and we agree that I have received every necessary immunization (see Immunity, page 118).

—————— **15.** I am aware of the need for hygienic behavior and have made it a part of my life (see Biological Stressors, page 30).

—————— **16.** I have reviewed my family history (see Genetic Stressors, page 110).

—————— **17.** I have discussed family/hereditary problems with my doctor (see Genetic Stressors, page 113).

—————— **18.** I am aware of my risk of developing familial/hereditary disorders and am prepared to minimize the risk with changes in my behavior.

—————— Total

The higher your score, the less likely you are to be involved in appropriate conditioning behavior. The following sections will help you to evaluate your needs more thoroughly and to develop your conditioning program.

We will begin to explore the methods of conditioning with exercise. Exercise may be defined as bodily exertion for the sake of keeping or restoring your organs and functions to a healthy state. There are at least four different types of exercise: stretching exercises, therapeutic exercises, conditioning exercises, and cardiovascular conditioning exercises. *Stretching exercises* are designed for loosening up or relaxing certain muscle groups. They are particularly useful for loosening up or relaxing tight muscles or muscles that have been injured. *Therapeutic exercises* are specifically designed to treat musculoskeletal disorders such as low back pain or weak knee ligaments. These are usually strengthening and stretching exercises that are designed to compensate for any of a number of pathological conditions of the musculoskeletal system. These exercises are prescribed by your physician if indicated. *Conditioning exercises* are designed to maintain or increase the strength of the muscles and/or to maintain joint flexibility and muscle tone. *Cardiovascular conditioning exercises* are designed to increase the fitness or capability of the heart and blood vessels to perform work. These are very vigorous exercises and are in themselves extremely stressful to the "unconditioned" heart. They must not be attempted without prior medical evaluation and must be done with great regularity and in a predictable manner.

PRESENT ACTIVITIES CHART

Please indicate which activities are included in your daily routine or in your daily exercise program.

Activity	Duration (number of minutes daily)	Frequency (number of times weekly)	Intensity (Effort)		
			MAXIMUM	MODERATE	MINIMUM
Walking					
Climbing stairs					
Running					
Swimming					
Tennis					
Racquetball					
Lifting heavy objects					
Cutting grass					
Chopping wood					

continued

Activity	Duration (number of minutes daily)	Frequency (number of times weekly)	Intensity (Effort)		
			MAXIMUM	MODERATE	MINIMUM
Shoveling					
Sweeping					
Other (please list)					

If you are seriously considering beginning an exercise program, you must learn the theory and procedure. Here are some basic rules, the details of which can be obtained by reading *The New Aerobics* by Kenneth H. Cooper, M.D. and *Stretching* by Bob Anderson.

1. Have a health evaluation done by your physician. Make sure you tell him or her that you intend to enter a vigorous exercise program. Do not deny any of your medical problems. *Tell him if you have any chest pain,* especially with activity. Follow your doctor's advice. If your doctor recommends a treadmill cardiogram prior to initiation of the program, do it. Once you have your doctor's OK, you can start.

2. Warm up slowly. There should be an approximately five-minute warm-up period. This usually includes calisthenics and/or walking while doing stretching exercises or breathing exercises.

3. Exercise to a peak heart rate which is your "submaximal" by the chart (p. 128). This phase of the exercise should be sustained for approximately 20 minutes minimum. Do not push yourself if you are feeling pain or extreme shortness of breath or exhaustion. Do not push yourself if you are sick. It is safer to keep your heart rate below the "submaximal" rates listed than to push your luck.

4. Cool down slowly. Do not just stop. A rapid halt is dangerous. (Stretching exercises can well be integrated into your cool-down period.)

5. Exercise at least three times weekly.

6. Do not exercise if you are sick.

7. Gradually increase the intensity of your exercise in order to maintain a "submaximal" heart rate for 20 minutes during your exer-

cise period. If you have missed a few days, back off to prior exercise levels and work back up. If you have exhausted yourself, take a few days off and start back at a less vigorous level. Sometimes a week off is therapeutic and will enhance future performance.

The following is a chart of "submaximal" heart rates which you can use as a guide for your exercise. They are rough estimates. If you are advised to proceed differently by your physician, do so.

Age	25	35	40	45	50	55	60	65
Heart Rate	140	132	128	124	119	115	111	107

FUTURE ACTIVITIES CHART

1. Please indicate which activities you wish to engage in as your regular form of exercise outside of work. Virtually any activity can be made into a form of exercise that will promote health and well-being.

Walking _____   Tennis _____

Running _____   Racquetball _____

Swimming _____   Other _____

_____

_____

_____

2. What alternative activities do you intend to use in the case of bad weather or other scheduling problems? _____

_____

3. Circle the three days of the week on which you plan to do your exercise:

Sunday   Monday   Tuesday   Wednesday   Thursday   Friday   Saturday

4. How much time do you plan to spend during each session? _____

Remember that for your exercise program you must have a *minimum* time of 5 minutes to warm up, 20 minutes of exercise to maintain the heart rate at 120 or above, and 5 minutes to cool down. If you are advised by your physician to keep your heart rate below 120, then you will probably have to extend the duration of the exercise. If you have been given a special program by your physician, do not alter it without his permission.

Motion is a normal and essential part of human behavior. Lack of motion (exercise/exertion) is an abnormal condition that results in the development of pathology (disease) or dysfunction. In other words, the body deteriorates without motion. Competitive exercise is not necessary to remain healthy. In fact, competitive exercise is likely to be detrimental except for those who are well trained and prepared specifically for competition. Exercise need not be painful in order to be beneficial. Exercise, when done properly, is a pleasant experience. In addition, it promotes well-being and health. Pain during exercise is often the result of improper intensity, duration, style, or clothing. You must begin your program of exercise gradually. You cannot make up for many years of inadequate activity by starting off your program at top speed. You cannot progress too slowly. Exercise which begins very slowly and progresses very gradually is *usually* safe for most people. Pain is neither an expected nor necessary part of your exercise program. Some types of pain during exercise are normal, although pain during exercise may need to be evaluated by your physician in order to exclude serious associated problems. You should begin to see and feel the effect of your exercise program within a short time. However, it does take several weeks to develop measurable improvement in cardiovascular fitness.

Do not give up; read and reread your references, and seek help if you are having problems. Remember to incorporate stretching exercises into your program of exercise. This is a very important factor in minimizing many of the complications of exercise.

Remember, exercise and all form of motion can be therapeutic. Exercise extinguishes the body's response to social and psychological stressors. However, excessive or inappropriate exercise may be more hazardous than you realize. Make sure you check with your physician before initiating an exercise program.

DIET AND NUTRITION

Food, as you will recall, is a major chemical-biological supporter. Adequate diet is essential to maintenance of proper bodily function. Without proper diet, other forms of conditioning are less effective; without proper diet, one cannot exercise effectively enough to maintain or improve condition; and without proper diet, the immune system fails to function properly, so that the immunizations provided by your physician and prior experience with infections will be less effective in preventing future infections. The following section will help you to explore your present eating behavior and plan for improvements in future eating.

Based on currently available information, the best all-around diet appears to be a high-protein, low-fat, low-carbohydrate diet. This consists primarily of eggs (one yolk daily), skimmed milk, fish, lean meat, fresh fruit, fresh vegetables, and whole grains. One serving of bread or its equivalent can be served at each meal. The bread/cereal should ideally be whole grain in order to maximize roughage (bulk). Vitamins *may* be added in reasonable amounts. Sweets should be saved for special occasions, and alcohol should be used in moderation (less than one ounce of absolute alcohol daily). *This diet is recommended only for healthy individuals with no known diseases that would contraindicate the diet.* Before you start such a diet, check with your physician and make sure that it is a reasonable one for you.

Foods consist of many chemicals (chemical supporters) derived from fresh or recently killed plants and animals or their fruit or eggs (biological supporters). The chemicals in food that are known to be beneficial include proteins, carbohydrates, fats, vitamins, and minerals. In order to be beneficial, these chemicals must be consumed in appropriate amounts for each individual. Both excesses and deficiencies may be harmful. Foods are known to be composed of varying proportions of the above-mentioned chemicals. Your diet consists of the combination of specific foods that you choose to consume.

It is impossible to provide a diet that would be adequate for everyone who reads this book. This is so because individual dietary requirements vary throughout the normal spectrum of health and illness that we see in the general population. In addition, the composition of foods changes depending on the specific conditions of their growth, preparation, and storage.

Nevertheless, this section will help you to explore your present eating behavior and plan for improvements in your future diet. Before you implement your planned dietary changes, check with your doctor to make sure that your plans are appropriate. He may wish to make certain modifications which will be of greater benefit to you.

In order to use this section to its maximum advantage, you will need to use a small kitchen scale so that you can fill in the charts accurately.

Carbohydrates

Carbohydrates are a basic group of organic chemicals found in both plants and animals. Carbohydrates are one of the most common chemical components of food. In plants, they function as a basic chemical both for energy storage and structure. They are one of the more common components of animal foodstuffs. Starches and sugars, including honey, comprise the majority of the commonly consumed carbohydrates and are found in many foods. In addition, a majority of the "bulk" or "roughage" foods which we eat are nondigestible carbohydrates (this does not mean that they will cause stomach or intestinal distress). Carbohydrates are processed (digested, absorbed, and metabolized) in the body and converted to glucose and/or glycogen and/or fat (primarily) and/or nonessential amino acids (those which can be manufactured in the body). A small amount of carbohydrate will promote maintenance of existing body protein. This effect (protein sparing) can be accomplished for the average adult by consuming approximately 100 grams of carbohydrate (a little more than three ounces) daily.

CARBOHYDRATE CONSUMPTION

Please fill out the following chart in order to measure your present carbohydrate consumption. Indicate the number of servings of each of the following which you eat in any average 24-hour period.

1 Food Type	2 Approximate Percentage of Carbohydrate	3 Serving Size (oz.)	4 Servings Daily	5 Daily Total (oz.) (col. 3 × col. 4)
Sugar, white	99			
Sugar, brown	96			
Sugar, maple	90			
Honey	82			
Molasses	65–70			
Cereal	80–90			
Candy	50–95			
Jam, jelly, preserves	70			

1	2	3	4	5
Food Type	Approximate Percentage of Carbohydrate	Serving Size (oz.)	Servings Daily	Daily Total (oz.) (col. 3 × col. 4)
Dried fruits	70			
Cookies	70			
Cakes	50–60			
Breads	50			
Pies	30–50			
Ice cream	20			
Carbonated beverages	10			
Grain products Cookies	70			
Cereals	80–90			
Cakes	50–60			
Breads	50			
Pancakes	50			
Waffles	50			
Wheat germ	47			
Macaroni (cooked)	20–30			
Nuts	15–20			
Vegetables Potatoes	20–30			
Rice	25			
Onions	6–10			
Corn	21			
Carrots (raw)	10			
Peas	12			
Artichokes	9.9			
Squash	3			
Peppers	5			
Tomatoes	5			
Other	—			
Fruit and fruit juice Berries	15			
Plums	15			

continued

	1	2	3	4	5
	Food Type	**Approximate Percentage of Carbohydrate**	**Serving size (oz.)**	**Servings Daily**	**Daily Total (oz.) (col. 3 × col. 4)**
	Figs	20			
	Pineapples	14			
	Bananas	22			
	Oranges	13			
	Grapefruits	10			
	Lemons	8			
	Green, leafy vegetables Lettuce	3			
	Celery	4			
	Spinach	4			
	All greens	5			
	Collards	5			
	Milk and milk products	5			
	Alcoholic beverages*				

Alcohol is not a carbohydrate, but it does contain calories with minimal associated food value i.e., no vitamins, minerals, protein, or fat. Some alcoholic beverages do contain carbohydrate also (e.g., beer is about 4% carbohydrate).

Now you can approximately calculate your total daily carbohydrate consumption by multiplying the weight of each daily total (column 5) by the percentage of carbohydrate in each food (column 2) and then adding up your results.† If your total exceeds 3⅓ ounces or 100 grams, you will probably be converting some carbohydrate to fat unless you exercise to use up the extra amount.

Carbohydrate consumption should be limited. The foods listed at the top of the preceding chart contain the highest percentage of carbohydrate per unit weight. The foods are listed in their approximate order of carbohydrate concentration as they would be used when prepared fresh or appropriately cooked without additional sweeteners. *Canned or otherwise processed foods cannot* be substituted in the same order as the freshly prepared foods given. Most canned fruits contain added sugar. You must read the label or consult a diet manual in order to compare the carbohydrate content of foods not listed. The refined or purified carbohydrates (sweets) have the least all-around nutritional value. They provide calories without providing other important nutrients. Sweets are virtually nutritionally worthless. (There are certain disease states for which doctors may prescribe a high-carbohydrate diet. Do not go against your doctor's instructions.) Alcoholic

†For example, to determine how much your drinking three 10-ounce glasses of milk each day adds to total daily carbohydrate intake, use the formula: 30 × 5/100 = 1.5 ounces of carbohydrates.

beverages, ice cream, cake, candy, pies, jams and jellies, sugar, and honey should be saved for special occasions and should then be consumed in limited quantities. Carbohydrate consumption should generally be limited to *unrefined,* fresh carbohydrates such as grains (bread and cereal), nuts, beans, fruits, and vegetables with no added sugar. Daily consumption of carbohydrate need not exceed one piece of whole grain bread or equivalent cereal and one piece of fresh fruit or serving of vegetables or its equivalent per meal, except when prescribed by your doctor, e.g., during times of illness.

For short periods of time when supplies dictate, fruits, vegetables, and grains may be substituted for each other in the following schedule for a total of six fruit/vegetable/grain/nut units in 24 hours. It should be noted that certain vegetables such as lettuce and celery have essentially no carbohydrate content (see vegetables in the section below on vitamins and minerals). These do not need to be included in your calculation of carbohydrate and can be eaten in any amount within reason. It is important to eat a variety of the unrefined carbohydrates in order to get maximum benefit from the roughage, protein, vitamins, and minerals that they contain.

Please refer back to the list of carbohydrates that you used for determination of your present consumption. List the top 10 carbohydrate foods that you are now consuming in order of the amount consumed (greatest weight first, least weight last).

1. _____   6. _____
2. _____   7. _____
3. _____   8. _____
4. _____   9. _____
5. _____   10. _____

Now review the list again and eliminate the refined carbohydrates. Make a new list of the top 10 carbohydrate foods that you have consumed after eliminating the refined carbohydrates.

1. _____   6. _____
2. _____   7. _____
3. _____   8. _____
4. _____   9. _____
5. _____   10. _____

How can you keep the refined carbohydrates out of your diet in the future? How can you keep your carbohydrate consumption down to approximately 3⅓ ounces? Think about a plan which you could use to implement these changes in your diet. You will be asked to review this material later in the book.

Fats

Fats are another group of organic chemicals commonly found in foods. They are a common component of animal meats, but are also found in relatively high proportions in certain parts of some plants (nuts and seeds). Fats function primarily as chemicals for energy storage. They are able to hold more energy per unit weight than either carbohydrate or protein and are therefore the body's most efficient form of energy storage. Fats are metabolized in the body to form body fat and are used in the production of work by muscles. In addition, they are used in the production of certain other essential body chemicals. Very little fat needs to be consumed in the diet, since most fats can be produced by the body from other food components. There are, however, a few fats called essential fats that must be consumed.

FAT CONSUMPTION

Please fill out the following chart. Indicate your present consumption of the following foods.

1	2	3	4	5
Food Type	Approximate Percentage of Fat	Serving Size (oz.)	Servings Daily	Daily Total (oz.) (col. 3 × col. 4)
Vegetable oil	100			
Lard, shortening	100			
Butter	81			
Margarine	81			
Mayonnaise	80			
Salad dressing (mayonnaise type)	42			
Nuts and seeds	50–60			
Bacon	52			
Sausage	44			
Salami	30			
Bologna	25			
Hot dogs	27			
Ham (leanest)	9			
Pork (leanest)	14			
Cheeses	30			
Cottage cheese	3–4			
Cream (heavy)	37			
Beef (choice, separable lean)	10			
Lamb	7			
Duck, goose (flesh only)	10			

continued

1	2	3	4	5
Food Type	Approximate Percentage of Fat	Serving Size (oz.)	Servings Daily	Daily Total (oz.) (col. 3 × col. 4)
Veal	10			
Chicken	5			
Nondairy creamers	(See label)			
Avocados	16			
Milk	3.5			
Eggs	11			
Fish	2–6			
Skimmed milk	0			

You can calculate the approximate total fat that you consume in an average day by multiplying the percentage fat for each food by the daily total for that food and dividing by 100. The sum of the results represents the approximate total fat that you consume. Fats contain approximately 9 calories per gram or 270 calories per ounce. If they are not used during exercise, they are readily converted to body fat.

Fat consumption should be limited. Essential fats will be obtained from your unavoidable fat consumption in the meat and vegetables that you eat. The foods listed in the previous chart are given in the order of the percentage of fat which they contain. Vegetable oil is 100 per cent fat and skimmed milk contains virtually none. The fat content of many of the listed meats is extremely variable and depends on the grade of meat (prime beef is higher than all other grades in fat content), the amount of fat removed in trimming, the cooking process and duration and heat of cooking, and the amount of trimming done at the table before consumption. The fat content of lean meats drops considerably after careful trimming and cooking if one is careful not to consume the fat. The calorie content of fat is higher than any other food type per unit weight and fat consumption is, therefore, a major contributor to the maintenance of overweight for many people. Fats also tend to be a storage depot for the accumulation of insecticides from the environment. The long-term effects of many are not known (see Chemical Stressors, page 21).

Please refer back to the list of fatty foods which you filled out previously. List the top 10 foods that you consume according to that list (by weight total).

1. _____   6. _____

2. _____   7. _____

3. _____   8. _____

4. _____   9. _____

5. _____   10. _____

How can you reduce your consumption of the fat contained in those foods listed above? Review your list and make a new list after eliminating the foods from the top 10 listed on the chart.

1. _____   6. _____
2. _____   7. _____
3. _____   8. _____
4. _____   9. _____
5. _____   10. _____

How can you further reduce your fat consumption?

All of the foods on the list can be part of your diet. They must, however, be consumed in a way that will limit your *total* fat consumption.

Fat consumption can be restricted to that which is unavoidable. In other words, wherever you can eliminate excess fat from your diet, you should do so. It is virtually impossible to consume an adequate diet without getting an adequate amount of fat including the essential fats.

Proteins

Proteins are nitrogen-containing organic chemicals composed of multiple smaller units—the amino acids. These chemicals, which again are found in both plants and animals, comprise much of the structural framework for animal cells and function in conjunction with vitamins and minerals as catalysts and enzymes. In addition, proteins form an essential component of the immune system, the blood-clotting system, and the endocrine (hormone) system, as well as others. Certain essential amino acids must be consumed by way of the protein in foods. Others can be manufactured in the body from other nonprotein chemicals. In order to maintain proper growth and function, adequate amounts of protein containing the proper mixture of amino acids must be consumed on a daily basis.

PROTEIN CONSUMPTION

In order to evaluate your present protein consumption, please fill out the following chart.

1 Food Type	2 Approximate Percentage of Protein	3 Serving Size (oz.)	4 Servings Daily	5 Daily Total (oz.) (col. 3 × col. 4)
Eggs	13			
Milk	6			
Bacon	34			
Chicken	34			

1	2	3	4	5
Food Type	Approximate Percentage of Protein	Serving Size (oz.)	Servings Daily	Daily Total (oz.) (col. 3 × col. 4)
Beef — Lean, no fat, broiled or roasted	30			
Duck	30			
Lamb	30			
Turkey	30			
Pork	30			
Ham	30			
Fish	25			
Seeds and peanuts	25			
Cheeses	15–25			
Shellfish	15			
Sausage	10			
Hot dogs	10			
Breads	10			
Beans	8			
Peas	3			
Rice	2.5			
Green vegetables	Virtually no protein			
Root vegetables				
Other vegetables				
Fruits				

Protein foods appear to be safe for virtually unlimited consumption by the healthy individual. There are certain individuals, however, with underlying predispositions to certain problems who may insidiously develop medical problems if they consume an unlimited amount of high-protein food. There are others with known pathology who absolutely cannot consume a high-protein diet. There are those who advocate a relatively small consumption of protein in the daily diet in order to avoid the development of these disorders. Although unlimited protein consumption cannot be advocated, there is excellent evidence to suggest that the general recommendations for protein consumption, while often adequate, are not optimum for all conditions of growth, development, and health maintenance. Protein requirements are based on the assumption that people are eating a significant percentage of "high-quality" proteins, that is, proteins originating from eggs, milk, meats, and liver. The quantity of protein required goes up as the quality of the protein consumed goes down. In addition, certain conditions of healing, growth, and development, as well as pregnancy and lactation, may dramatically increase dietary protein requirements (nearly four times).

The recommended daily protein requirement is approximately 1/1000 of a person's (healthy adult) body weight. This would be approximately 0.15 pounds of high-quality *protein* for a healthy 150-pound adult, or the equivalent of a minimum of approximately 10 eggs daily or eight ounces of lean meat or fish. The diet should contain a variety of high-protein foods, including some with "high-quality" proteins. Meats should be lean, and all separable fat should be trimmed off. Vegetarians should eat some eggs or milk or else must make special accommodations in their diet to allow for the lower quality of the proteins in vegetables. Those with special health problems and/or di-

---

CALCULATING YOUR TOTAL DAILY PROTEIN CONSUMPTION

Please refer back to the chart of proteins which you previously filled out. List the protein foods that you are presently consuming with the percentage protein in the column next to it (by weight total).

Food Type (1)	Percentage Protein (2)	Approximate Daily Amount = Consumed × Protein (%) (3)	Approximate Protein (by weight) (4)
Eggs	13	(oz. × 13/100)	
Milk	6	(oz. × 6/100)	
Bacon	34	(oz. × 34/100)	
Chicken	34	(oz. × 34/100)	
Beef	30	(oz. × 30/100)	
Duck	30	(oz. × 30/100)	
Lamb	30	(oz. × 30/100)	
Turkey	30	(oz. × 30/100)	
Pork	30	(oz. × 30/100)	
Ham	30	(oz. × 30/100)	
Fish	25	(oz. × 25/100)	
Seeds and peanuts	25	(oz. × 25/100)	
Cheese	15–25	(oz. × 20/100)	
Shellfish	15	(oz. × 15/100)	
Sausage	10	(oz. × 10/100)	
Hot dogs	10	(oz. × 10/100)	
Bread	10	(oz. × 10/100)	
Beans	8	(oz. × 8/100)	
Peas	3	(oz. × 3/100)	
Rice	2.5	(oz. × 2.5/100)	
Green vegetables*	—	(oz. × 0)	0

continued

Food Type (1)	Percentage Protein (2)	Approximate Daily Amount = Consumed × Protein (%) (3)	Approximate Protein (by weight) (4)
Root vegetables*	—	(oz. × 0)	0
Other vegetables*	—	(oz. × 0)	0
Fruits*	—	(oz. × 0)	0

†Total ounces *protein* = _____
(sum of col. 4)

Total ounces protein ÷ 16 = Total pounds protein = _____

Total pounds protein × 1000 = _____

*These foods contain virtually no protein.
†It should be made very clear that total protein consumed is not equal to the weight of the meat or fish or other high protein food consumed. Weight of food type must be multiplied by percentage of protein in order to get the actual weight of the protein consumed.

etary needs (pregnancy, lactation, and illness) should follow their doctor's dietary instructions.

If your protein consumption in pounds × 1000 is greater than your proper weight, and you eat some milk and/or eggs, then you are probably eating enough protein.

If your consumption × 1000 exceeds your weight by greater than 50 percent and you are healthy, then you should ask your doctor if you should cut down on protein consumption. If your consumption is low, check with your doctor to see if it should be increased.

Vitamins and Minerals

Vitamins are a collection of organic chemicals that are essential in small quantities in the diet. Minerals are crystalline inorganic chemicals which are variably soluble in liquids. Certain minerals are essential in the diet (trace minerals). Vitamins and minerals appear to function primarily in the metabolism of other chemicals in the body; in other words, vitamins and minerals facilitate the processing of other chemicals contained in food and in the elimination of environmental poisons and waste products of normal growth and development and body maintenance.

Vitamins and minerals are found in all foods and most water. The use of supplementary synthetic or natural vitamin pills remains a controversial subject. However, despite the controversy, there appears to be no harm in supplementing a diet adequate in food-contained vitamins with *water-soluble* vitamins (B and C). In addition, certain of the fat-soluble vitamins (vitamin E) appear to be harmless. Vitamins A and D, however, are potentially toxic in high doses and are not necessary in supplements for adults. Vitamin supplements are not a substitute for a proper diet. Fresh foods may contain many as yet unidentified essential nutrients which are not contained in vitamin pills.

VITAMIN CONSUMPTION			
Please fill out the following questionnaire in order to determine your present consumption of vitamins and minerals in fresh foods.			
1	2	3	4
Food Type	**Serving Size (oz.)**	**Servings Daily**	**Daily Total (oz.) (col. 2 × col. 3)**
High-carbohydrate vegetables Potatoes			
Onions			
Beans			
Corn			
Peas			
Other			
Low-carbohydrate vegetables Lettuce			
Celery			
Carrots			
Broccoli			
Cauliflower			
Spinach			
Other greens			
Squash			
Pumpkin			
Green beans			
Brussel sprouts			
Eggplant			
Tomatoes			
Cucumbers			
Artichokes			
Asparagus			
Other			
Nuts and seeds			
Grain products Breads			
Cereal			
Other			
Fresh fruits			

continued

Food Type	Serving Size (oz.)	Servings Daily	Daily Total (oz.) (col. 2 × col. 3)
Meat			
Fish			
Cheese			
Eggs			
Other			

A diet that contains the foods previously discussed in the proper amounts and a liberal amount of raw and cooked fresh low-carbohydrate vegetables will probably contain adequate amounts of vitamins and minerals for the average healthy adult. Remember, though, that cooking and canning of the foods will probably reduce their vitamin content. Certain stressful conditions will increase vitamin requirements. Supplementary water-soluble vitamins, though not always necessary, will probably help to maintain adequate levels of vitamins even when the requirements rise. If you wonder whether or not to take a vitamin supplement, and what to take, discuss it with your doctor.

Special Dietary Considerations

The preceding material on diet should not be looked upon as a complete dietary program. It should rather be taken as a brief guide or introduction to the principles of proper eating. The following material should help you to begin to make decisions about other aspects of your diet.

1. *Food additives and preservatives* (artificial colors, artificial sweeteners, spices, artificial flavors, preservatives, flavor enhancers, emulsifiers, etc.). These are commonly used chemicals. The health effects of most of them are virtually unknown. However, certain of those previously thought to be safe have been confirmed as either creating definite or potential health problems. The controversial banning of certain additives with no "proven" adverse effects and the lack of proof for or against the use of most food additives serves only to confuse the public. The fact is that food additives are chemicals, most of which have not been "proven" to be safe. They usually can be avoided with minimal effort. You have the choice. If you want to avoid them, you merely have to read the labels on food items you purchase. You can assume that every food has additives until proven otherwise. You must be selective.

2. *Table salt.* This commonly used chemical (sodium chloride) was originally used as a preservative. It remains in common use along with other spices. While this practice probably has no adverse effects for most people, there is some evidence to suggest that long-term addition of salt to food may be a contributing factor in the development of hypertension (increased blood pressure). Avoidance of salt is considered a hardship by many people. However, once salt is dropped from the diet, adjustment to its absence is rapid. Within a few weeks, you will begin to appreciate the real taste of your food.

3. *Food preservation.* Careful consideration of food preservation should be a critical part of your dietary routine. Heating and cooling remain important in preserving food quality. Certain chemicals (preservatives) are added to retard spoilage. The consumption of spoiled foods can result in major health consequences ranging from intoxication to infection to death. *Do not eat any questionable food.* If you think it is bad, throw it out.

4. *Cholesterol.* The subject of dietary cholesterol consumption remains controversial. For certain individuals, it appears to be necessary to keep consumption of it to a minimum. Your doctor must advise you on this matter.

5. *Toxic chemicals and fat.* Many toxic chemicals are ingested through the consumption of animal fat in milk, butter, cheese, and meats. These chemicals are, in turn, stored in the body fat of human beings. Little is known about the health effects of these stored toxins. During lactation (breast-feeding), these fats and toxic chemicals may be mobilized and found in increased concentrations in breast milk. This is known to be true of certain insecticides and drugs. The effects of these chemicals on the nursing infant are largely unknown. However, some are known to be detrimental, especially to the developing fetus and newborn baby.

6. *Obesity.* Although this is a common health problem, little specific advice will be provided in this book for the obese individual. If obesity (overweight) is a problem for you, you will need to get specific advice from your doctor regarding this issue. However, many people, for a variety of reasons, see themselves as overweight when they really are not. If you are not measurably overweight and you think you are obese, reread the section on attitude and self-esteem or seek professional help. For most normal weight and moderately overweight individuals, the suggestions given in this book will probably be approved by your doctor.

7. *Fad diets.* Weight control is a life-long proposition requiring proper eating behavior. Any diet that does not emphasize the fact that a long-term change is necessary is unlikely to work. Starvation diets may be extremely dangerous and should be avoided. Long-term dietary deprivation produces malnutrition that may exceed the risk of being overweight. Social pressures often cause people to go on repeated starvation diets. This is an unhealthy practice and often leads to increased weight and fat gain.

Nutrition

Diet is one of the most difficult health behaviors to give advice on. Even though people have been eating for a long time, the study of nutrition is an infant science which is based on the study of only the most obvious occurrences of the major diseases that result from dietary deficiencies. All of the recommended daily requirements are based on the minimum quantities of each nutrient that will prevent deficiency diseases in most of the people of a certain age under average circumstances. In other words, some individuals may require more of certain nutrients and others less. Under certain normal but extreme conditions, some requirements definitely increase (e.g., during pregnancy and lactation). Under other circumstances, they decrease. Certain inherited disorders of metabolism may drastically alter the requirements of the various nutrients (e.g., disorders of fat, carbohydrate, and protein metabolism). In other words, dietary intake recommendations remain controversial.

The purpose of the diet remains the attainment and maintenance of health. Diet is obviously not the sole factor in health, and due to the lack of scientific evidence, it is impossible to give a general diet that is suitable for every individual. However, this book will provide you with the basic information you will need to initiate your dietary improvements. Check with your doctor before initiating any changes.

If your physician agrees that a high-protein, low-carbohydrate, low-fat, high-bulk diet is appropriate for you, he will be able to provide you with an instruction sheet which will include sample menus and more complete food lists than are supplied in this book.

FUTURE FOOD CONSUMPTION INSTRUCTIONS					
Please use the following chart to plan your first week of eating your new diet. List the foods you plan to eat			in each category and the approximate weight (in ounces). Review this plan with your physician.		
	Food Components				
	Protein	**Fat**	**Carbohydrate**	**Vitamins* + Minerals**	**Roughage**
Sun.					
Mon.					
Tues.					
Wed.					
Thurs.					
Fri.					
Sat.					

In food.

In addition to the previously discussed conditioning factors of exercise motion, diet and nutrition, there are additional health behaviors that affect you. Those previously covered are cross-referenced.

1. *Immunization.* An immunization list has already been presented for your use. Review your immunization deficiencies and check with your doctor to make sure you are taking advantage of this important and effective conditioning mode.

2. *Hygiene.* Hygienic behavior has been reviewed under the checklist following the section on Biological Stressors. (page 29.) Return now to that section in Chapter 3 and review your deficiencies. Make a plan to incorporate hygienic behavior into your future lifestyle.

3. *Risk Reduction.* Risk reduction is accomplished through avoidance of stressors and maintaining healthful behavior. However, there are certain problems which can only be detected by your physician and which appear to be influenced favorably by early recognition and treatment. These include certain inherited disorders of fat and carbohydrate metabolism, which, if detected early, appear to cause fewer problems later on. Check with your doctor in order to determine your need for this type of evaluation.

METHODS OF RELAXATION

Relaxation may be defined as the process of lessening tension. Relaxation methods increase stress tolerance by allowing us to remove ourselves temporarily from the need to accomplish any tasks. They allow us to extinguish our body's response to stress. They tend to be refreshing and to improve our perspective and ability to accomplish our tasks once we are back at them.

SCALE 19–METHODS OF RELAXATION					
Indicate the frequency with which you make use of the relaxation methods presented in the following list.					
5	4	3	2	1	X
Never	**Rarely**	**Weekly**	**Daily**	**Many Times Daily**	**Unknown**

_____ **1.** Meditation

Comment: _____

_____

_____ **2.** Deep-muscle relaxation

Comment: _____

_____

_____ **3.** Self-hypnosis

Comment: _____

_____

continued

5	4	3	2	1	X
Never	**Rarely**	**Weekly**	**Daily**	**Many Times Daily**	**Unknown**

4. Yoga

Comment: _____

5. Biofeedback

Comment: _____

6. Exercise

Comment: _____

7. Vacations

Comment: _____

8. Recreation

Comment: _____

9. Hobbies

Comment: _____

10. Music

Comment: _____

11. Other

_____

Total

The higher the score, the more you need to establish a program of relaxation. In the next several pages, you will be examining some of these methods in more detail. Hobbies, music, recreation, and vacations are self-explanatory and will not be discussed in this book.

Biofeedback

There are several unconscious body responses which can be "fed back" to the user through the use of rather simple electronic devices. They include muscle tension, heart rate, blood pressure, skin resistance, brain waves, and others. Through the use of these painless electronic machines, these body functions can be observed as they change in quality or intensity. This is called *biofeedback.*

Biofeedback is used for enhancement of one's ability to deal with stress. It should not be used in isolation and is most effective when used under professional supervision. It is a method whereby normally unconscious and automatic body responses can be measured and displayed in such a way as to encourage or discourage these responses in the user.

The measurement and display of information concerning an individual's muscle tension (electromyography, EMG) is an important adjunct in learning relaxation techniques (muscle tension frequently rises in response to stress). This method measures the minute electrical charge on the surface of the muscle that accompanies the maintenance of tension within a muscle. This is a normal side effect of muscular contraction; that is, as the muscle contracts or tightens, the surface of the muscle exhibits increasing electrical charge. Normally, one has to concentrate very carefully in order to recognize his or her own muscular tension. And indeed, some people have no awareness of their own muscle tension. However, with the aid of EMG set up for "feedback," people can rapidly learn to recognize the muscular tension and then learn to relax that tension.

The procedure is simple, safe, and painless. Three surface electrodes are placed on the forehead. They are attached through wires to the electronic device designed to measure the very small units of electricity that come from the frontalis muscle underlying the skin of the forehead. The device is battery-powered and cannot give you an electric shock.

Other types of biofeedback used for relaxation training include measurements of changes in electrical potential on the skin (Galvanic Skin Response, GSR) and measurements of brain waves. Some people do not experience muscular tension when under stress, but become viscerally aroused. The galvanic skin response helps such "gut responders" to learn to relax these outwardly invisible symptoms of stress. Certain brain waves, particularly alpha waves, are associated with relaxed, peaceful sensations. By learning to produce alpha waves at will, an individual can learn to enhance his state of relaxation. Monitoring brain-wave functions is helpful for individuals who respond to stress by becoming confused or disoriented rather than muscularly or internally aroused.

Deep-Muscle Relaxation/Self-Hypnosis

This technique is an extremely useful method to lessen the effects of stress if you are the kind of person who experiences backaches, tension headaches, or muscle tension as a response to pressure. For many of us who respond this way, our normal state of muscular tension may be moderately high, so that we come to think of that as "relaxed" and "normal." We do not know when we are getting tense, only when we have arrived at an uncomfortable state. We are unaware of the gradual process. We may certainly know when we become "uptight" but not know where our body is being affected or how to reduce muscular tension.

This training will consist of three sections. In the first section, you will learn to identify by sensation the major muscle groups in your body and become familiar with the feeling of tension in just those muscles. You will then learn how to relax just those muscles. The series of exercises will have you alternately tense and then relax different muscles to sensitize you to their location and to demonstrate how you can relax localized parts of your body. The second section of training will help you to put into practice your new ability to relax through a series of relaxation suggestions and breathing exercises. The third section will give you additional methods of relaxing and deepening relaxation through self-hypnotic suggestions. You will be asked to imagine scenes in a way that will lead to a deep sense of comfort.

These instructions can be read verbatim to an individual or group, preferably by someone already familiar with muscle relaxation; the learning will be valuable even if a skilled trainer is not available.*

(To be read very slowly and quietly)

A majority of people do not know when they are getting tense. They may know they are tense, but they do not recognize the gradual process in terms of their musculature. The first point in teaching muscle relaxation is to learn to identify different muscle groups and what they feel like when they are tense and then to pay attention to what you do to relax them. I cannot tell you how to relax your muscles, but in practicing, you will discover your own way of doing it. Then you will be able to repeat this procedure yourself. If that does not make sense to you at the moment, it will in a few more minutes. The first step in teaching muscle relaxation involves a series of exercises where you alternately tense, then relax different muscle groups. In a sense it tells you where those muscles are and teaches you how to loosen them up. Later on, you will not have to go through tensing the muscle when you want to relax. All you will do is run a mental check through your body, locate where the tension is and relax the muscle(s). You can use this in a variety of ways. You can sit down for 10 or 20 minutes daily and go through this procedure. You can use it any time during the day, any place you are, to mentally check your body, find the tension, and relax within a few seconds' time. Sometimes, muscular tension produces discomfort that in itself leads to more anxiety and tension. This relaxation technique breaks that cycle. You can also use it to fall asleep at night.

Make yourself as comfortable as you can and shut your eyes.

(Reader, wait 10″–15″.)†

The first thing to do is to explore the different muscle groups in the body. The purpose in doing so will be to sensitize yourself to what those muscles feel like when they are tense and how you relax them. Start by working on the muscles in your head, the major source of tension headaches. Let your attention focus on your forehead and your scalp. (Wait 10″–15″) . . . Now tense those muscles, *frown*, and pay attention to where you feel the sensation. Go ahead and *frown* hard, but be careful not to produce pain. Feel the tension, but stop short of discomfort. . . (wait 5″) . . . now relax, let it all go loose . . . (wait 10″) . . . Start getting used to dealing with the contrast to know when those muscles are tense and relaxed, and what you do to relax them. Frown again . . . (wait 5″) . . . relax. You may have found that it takes several seconds for the muscles to smooth out. Sometimes they relax all at once and sometimes they gradually loosen. One more time, tense . . . (wait 5″) . . . relax. (Wait 10″.)
(Wait 10″.)

Now I want you to focus your attention on your jaw. A lot of people under pressure clench their teeth, and this results in painful problems with the jaw muscles, teeth grinding, and tension headaches. I want

---

*Relaxation tapes are available from a variety of sources, including the authors.
†Seconds are designated by ″. These are suggested times and, although not magical, should be roughly adhered to. You may lengthen the relaxation times, but don't try to speed up the procedure. Any exercise may be repeated as often as necessary.

you to clench your jaw really tight. Pay attention to where you feel tension. Is there tension in your forehead or running down your neck? Now relax. When your mouth is really relaxed, it hangs open about a quarter of an inch. If your teeth are touching you are not completely relaxed. Let your mouth hang open. One more time, tense . . . (wait 5″) . . . relax. (Wait 10″.)

Now shift your attention to the muscles in your neck. I want you to imagine someone has his hand on your forehead. In a moment I am going to ask you to *try* to push against that hand. You are not going to be able to move it, but go ahead and try. Tense . . . Pay attention to the pattern of tense muscles . . . relax. What are you doing to relax those muscles? Again, tense . . . (wait 5″) . . . relax. Now imagine that someone's hand is at the back of your head. I am going to ask you to press against that. Tense . . . (wait 5″) . . . relax . . . (wait 5″) . . . tense . . . (wait 5″) . . . relax. Now I want you to try to push forward and back at the same time. Tense . . . (wait 5″) . . . relax.

(Wait 10″.)

Now I am going to ask you to try and move your shoulders up to touch your ears. Tense . . . (wait 5″) . . . relax, let it all go . . . (wait 10″) . . . again tense . . . (wait 5″) . . . and relax . . . (wait 10″). Now I am going to ask you to try to move your shoulders backward as if they could meet at your spine. Tense . . . (wait 5″) . . . let it go, relax . . . (wait 10″) . . . tense . . . (wait 5″) . . . relax.

(Wait 10″.)

Let your attention shift to your hands. Adjust your arms so the palms are upward. When I tell you to, I want you to clench your fists Clench now. Pay attention to what other muscles are being affected. Now relax . . . (wait 10″) . . . tense again . . . (wait 5″) . . . now relax. Let your hands go limp. Enjoy the contrast, enjoy the relaxation.

(Wait 10″.)

Now imagine someone is holding your wrists down and you cannot move them. I want you to try to shift your hands. Tense. Pay attention. Where else do you feel tension? . . . Relax. Tense . . . (wait 5″) . . . and relax.

(Wait 10″.)

I want you to work on your abdominal muscles for a moment. I want you to imagine that someone is about to punch you right in the gut. Your only protection is to tighten those muscles as much as you can to ward off the blow. Now, tense. Take a look at what happens to your breathing . . . (wait 5″) . . . relax . . . (wait 10″) . . . one more time, tense . . . (wait 5″) . . . and relax.

(Wait 10″.)

Now you are going to work on your legs, and soon I will show you how to put it all together. Imagine that someone is pushing down on your knees. I am going to ask you to *try* to raise your knees against that pressure. Go ahead, tense . . . (wait 5″) . . . relax . . . (wait 10″) . . . again . . . tense . . . (wait 5″) . . . relax.

(Reader, read very slowly, calmly.)

Now let us put what you have learned about relaxing into practice. First, make a guess about how tense you are right now. On a scale from 1 to 10, where 1 is as relaxed as you have ever been and 10 is as tense as possible.

Where do you rate yourself now?

(Wait 10″.)

Now listen.

I will name different parts of your body, and as I do so, let your attention focus on those body parts. If you notice any tension, try to relax the muscles. If all the tension does not disappear, do not worry. Just try to reduce the tensions you feel. Now, let your mind focus on your forehead and scalp, relax these muscles . . . (wait 5″) . . . relax . . . relax the muscles in your jaw . . . (wait 5″) . . . relax the muscles in your neck . . . (wait 5″) . . . let your head hang down limp . . . (wait 5″) . . . relax the muscles in your hands . . . (wait 5″) . . . let your arms hang completely limp. Relax the muscles in your shoulders . . . (wait 5″) . . . relax the muscles in your chest . . . (wait 5″) . . . abdomen . . . (wait 5″) . . . relax the muscles in your buttocks . . . (wait 5″) . . . in your thighs . . . (wait 5″) . . . calves . . . (wait 5″) . . . your feet . . . (wait 5″) . . . just enjoy being relaxed.

(Reader, wait 15″–20″.)

As you remain relaxed with your eyes closed, I am going to begin to count from 1 to 10. Imagine that with each count a wave of relaxation like a wave rolling across a beach is sweeping over your body from your head through your torso down to your feet. The more you imagine it, the more you will feel it and the deeper your relaxation will become . . . one . . . (wait 5″) . . . a wave of relaxation is flowing through your body . . . (wait 5″) . . . two, *more* and *more* relaxed . . . three, imagine the relaxation rolling like a wave through your body; (wait 5″) four, *deeper* and *deeper;* (wait 5″) five, so relaxed; (wait 5″) six, *deeper* and *deeper;* (wait 5″) seven, *deeper;* (wait 5″) eight, down, down; (wait 5″) nine, (wait 5″) ten, *deeper* and *deeper* still . . . (wait 10″). Now I want you to continue this on your own. I want you to count in your mind from one to ten, with each count becoming more and more relaxed. Go ahead, lift an index finger to let me know when you are finished counting.

(Reader, wait.)

Now I am going to show you another technique that you can use to deepen your relaxation. Imagination is an extraordinarily powerful thing. The more you imagine something, the more it seems to be real. Follow these suggestions and you will be very pleasantly surprised. Keep your eyes closed, your body relaxed, and follow the instructions.

(Reader, very slowly, repetitively)

Now, I want you to imagine some place that you have been where it was peaceful, beautiful, restful. It may be a real place. It may be a place in your imagination. Someplace you can go in your mind that is relaxing to you and makes you feel peaceful and tranquil. Imagine it vividly. Enjoy your private and relaxing fantasy. Go ahead and escape in your dream. I will talk to you again in a short while.

(Wait 2 to 5 minutes.)

Listen to my voice now. In a few moments, I will help you wake up. Keep your eyes closed and, inside your head, silently and slowly begin to count backward from 10 to 1. As you count you will gradually begin to awaken so that when you reach the count of 1, you will open your eyes, feel very relaxed, peaceful, tranquil, and alert. Do not move around right away, take your time . . . Begin to count in your head from 10 to 1.

(Wait until all participants are awake.)

When all eyes are open, ask, "How tense are you now on the 1 to 10 scale?"

EXPLANATION AND PRACTICE INSTRUCTIONS. You did several things. The tensing and relaxing preliminary exercise was just to sensitize you to where your muscles are located. When practicing this over the next week, tense and relax just for a few minutes each time until you become aware of exactly where your muscles are located. If you have problems with headaches, focus on your head. If you have problems with your back, focus more on those muscles. If your muscles do tend to respond to stress, which muscle groups? Find someplace comfortable, close your eyes, let your mind go right through your body, relaxing the tension as you find it; count from 1 to 10 to relax some more.

There are three different techniques involved in this exercise. Deep-muscle relaxation is relaxing the body. Imagining a pleasant fantasy is a form of meditation/self-hypnosis. You can use them all in combination or you can use any one of them individually, whatever is useful for you. This is something that you have control over and that you can do entirely on your own. You can stop anytime you wish. This is a skill; the more you practice it, the better you will be able to do it and the more good you will get out of it.

Meditation

People have been practicing ways to get into a state of relaxation since the beginning of time, and there are probably a thousand different ways to meditate. This type of meditation is a way for you to focus inward that produces deep relaxation and also energizes you. In 20 minutes of good meditation, you can actually get the equivalent of a couple of hours of sleep. There has been substantial research done on this form of meditation. When you meditate, your body's metabolism slows down. You are not asleep, your mind stays alert, but your body goes into a state of deep relaxation, your heart rate slows down, your breathing slows down, and your blood pressure decreases. The effect is that your body gets a lot of intense relaxation, so that during the rest of the day you feel more energized. Because you are more rested, you tend to be less tense, less cranky, your head is clearer, and you can even think more clearly and generally feel better.

The method we will show you is simple, easy, and effective. Make yourself comfortable. A semireclining position is good; try not to lie down. (Sleep is not your goal.) Close your eyes and pay attention to what you feel in your body, what sensations you are aware of. Keep your eyes closed, and watch what happens to your body. (Wait 60".) Now open your eyes. What did you notice happened to your body as you sat with your eyes closed? Your breathing began to slow down. There were other changes that you might not have noticed: your heart rate probably started to slow down; your blood pressure started to drop. Human beings display a *relaxation response* such that when you sit down and are quiet and close your eyes, your body automatically begins to relax. When you meditate, always start with a short period of sitting still and closing your eyes to let that automatic relaxation response begin. About a minute after your body has had a chance to unwind, begin to pay attention to your breathing. Each time you breathe out say, in your head, the letter *O*.* Repeat it in your head over and over, each time you exhale, over and over and over again. What seems to happen when you do this is that the part of your mind that worries and obsesses seems to turn down and even shuts off. What

---

*Some people get uncomfortable when thinking about their breathing. If this bothers you, just repeat the letter *O* over and over again in your head during the meditation.

is left may be some thoughts, fantasies, or perhaps a blank period when you are not aware of anything in particular. You will find as you meditate that you will cycle in and out, in and out, from thinking to not being aware of thinking, to thinking, and then not thinking. This form of meditation involves no work, no concentration. This may sound strange, but after you have experienced it for a few minutes, this will become clear to you. Do not sit there and say to yourself "I've got to focus on *O*, I've got to focus on *O*." This is work. That is not meditating. Simply focus on your breathing and silently say *"O"* on each exhalation. What will happen is that you think a while, and then you will realize that you have not been thinking or you have been daydreaming; maybe you have been asleep. Whenever you become aware that you are not focused on *O* and your breathing, just refocus and you will drift on and off, on and off. That is exactly what is supposed to happen. You do not have to sit there and concentrate. Just think about your breathing when you are aware of it, and when you realize you have forgotten, think about it again. While your brain is doing this, your body is getting a period of deep relaxation. It is going to leave you feeling much better.

When you wake yourself up from your meditation, *do not* open your eyes right away. Do *not* move about right away. Take your time waking up. Take up to several minutes if you wish. When you want to awaken from your meditation, do the following: Stop focusing on your breathing, stop listening for the letter *O*. Instead, direct your attention to the sounds around you. Wait at least two or three minutes before moving. Recall how uncomfortable you have felt when waking suddenly from a deep sleep. If you move quickly after meditating, you might experience similar responses. Take your time.

During your meditation, you may experience some of the following sensations.

1. The sense of time often becomes distorted while meditating, the predominant experience being that only a few minutes have gone by, when in reality the time has been considerably longer.

2. Some people have a tendency to try to *concentrate,* to *force* themselves to focus their attention on their breathing and away from thoughts. This is a mistake. This approach to meditating involves *no effort.* Thoughts during this type of meditation are normal. The rule is that when you become aware of thoughts, simply refocus on your breathing.

3. You may have found that you did not relax as much as you expected. Each time you meditate, the experience will be somewhat different. The best way to approach it is to have no expectations other than that your body will have 20 minutes to rest. The meditation process will then take care of itself. Sometimes, you will barely unwind before the 20 minutes are up. Other times, the 20 minutes will seem like 5 and you will have no recollection of what happened to you.

4. To get the full impact from this technique, you ought to do it twice a day for 20 minutes. How do you know when 20 minutes have elapsed? Do not use an alarm clock. Have a wrist watch or a clock in front of you and from time to time, open your eyes and check the time. If the time is up, close your eyes again, listen to the sounds in the room until you feel like moving and then get up. If

20 minutes are not up, close your eyes, focus on your breathing, and go back to meditating again. After several practice sessions, your body will automatically know when 20 minutes have elapsed and will start to wake up.

5. Where and when you meditate is important. If other people are in the house or office, you need to let them know what you are doing and ask them to stay away from you. Most people find that meditating is most helpful sometime around midmorning and again late in the afternoon (before meals). That is when you really need energizing. Do not do it just before you go to sleep. If it energizes you, then you will be awake and unable to fall asleep. Meditation is not designed to help you go to sleep, but to give you energy and peace of mind. One reason people get edgy, jumpy, and do not think clearly is that they are exhausted. If you have been under emotional pressure for some time, you are going to be exhausted. Even when the pressure starts to let up, you are still tired. The more regularly you meditate, twice a day, 20 minutes at a time, seven days a week, the more you will begin to notice a difference. Meditation has a cumulative effect; once a day is better than none, twice a day is much better than once a day. Medical research indicates that twice a day is sufficient; more is not necessarily better and may, in fact, be harmful.

Recreation and Hobbies

Play is a critical activity in the maintenance of good physical and emotional health. All work and no play can make you feel and be dull. Fill in the following chart to assess how well you treat yourself in this area.

RECREATION AND HOBBIES				
List at Least 10 Activities or Hobbies That You Enjoy.	How Often Do You Participate in It?	When Was the Last Time You Did It?	When Will You Do It Again? Who Do You Need To Help You Do This?	What Excuse Do You Give Yourself for Not Doing This More Often?

5
Implementing Change

SUMMARIZING YOUR STRESSORS AND SUPPORTERS

Below is a summary of internal and environmental stressors and supporters that you may be experiencing. List or check those which you have found pertain to you. Please review the appropriate checklists from Chapter 3 and list your major problem areas by highest scores. This will enable you to begin a plan of action to reduce your susceptibility and increase your tolerance to stress.

CHECKLIST OF STRESSORS AND SUPPORTERS

Environmental Stressors (see page 15)

1. Physical (page 16)
   _____   _____
   _____   _____
   _____   _____
   _____   _____

2. Chemical (page 21)
   _____   _____
   _____   _____
   _____   _____
   _____   _____

3. Biological (page 29)
   _____   _____
   _____   _____
   _____   _____
   _____   _____

4. Social (page 34)
   _____   _____
   _____   _____
   _____   _____
   _____   _____

Internal Stressors (see page 40)

1. Attitudinal (p. 40)

_____   My need for approval from others is too high.

_____   My need for achievement is too high and/or too unrealistic.

_____   My self-concept needs to be improved.

_____   I tend to be a workaholic.

_____   My wish to control everything and everyone around me is unrealistic.

_____   My sense of control over important parts of my life is too low.

_____   Others

2. Behavioral (page 56)

_____   _____

_____   _____

_____   _____

_____   _____

3. Genetic (List diseases which run in your family.) (page 110)

_____   _____

_____   _____

_____   _____

4. Immunological (List your immunization deficiencies.) (page 118)

_____   _____

_____   _____

_____   _____

5. Pathological (List your known diseases and disabilities.) (page 120)

_____   _____

_____   _____

_____   _____

_____   _____

Interpersonal Stressors (see page 68)

_____   I am overdemanding and nongiving.

_____   I am too self-sacrificing.

_____   My communication skills need improvement.

_____   I need to learn to listen better.

_____   I need to be more assertive and constructively confronting.

_____   Inadequate support network

_____   Inappropriate responses to anger

_____   Others

continued

Situational Stressors (see pages 98–99)

1. Task and Role stress

_____   I am experiencing difficulty in relationships with people at work.

_____   I am experiencing difficulty in relationships with people in my family.

_____   I have too much or too little work to do on the job.

_____   I have too much or too little work to do at home.

_____   What I am expected to do on the job is not clearly understood and is causing me stress.

_____   What I am expected to do at home is not clearly agreed upon and is a cause of pressure for me.

_____   Others

2. Current and recent life events and changes (see pages 100, 104, 107).

_____

_____

_____

_____

_____

_____

_____

_____

3. My current life stage and my reaction to this stage in my development (see page 107).

_____

_____

_____

_____

_____

_____

_____

Environmental Supporters

1. Physical (page 20)   _____   _____

_____   _____

_____   _____

_____   _____

2. Chemical (page 28)   _____   _____

_____   _____

_____   _____

continued

3. Biological (page 33) _____ _____

_____ _____

_____ _____

4. Social (pages 37, 64) _____ _____

_____ _____

_____ _____

_____ _____

Internal Supporters

1. Attitudinal (page 41*) _____ _____

_____ _____

_____ _____

_____ _____

2. Behavioral (page 70) _____ _____

_____ _____

_____ _____

_____ _____

3. Genetic (page 114) _____ _____

_____ _____

_____ _____

_____ _____

4. Immunological (page 116) _____ _____

_____ _____

_____ _____

_____ _____

*You can extend this checklist by using a yellow pad and referring back to the sections on Interpersonal Style: Supporters (pages 64–66) and Task- and Role-Based Stress (pages 98–99) or by making subdivisions of any other areas that are of particular interest.

HOW TO FEEL BETTER MORE OF THE TIME AND REDUCE YOUR CHANCES OF A MAJOR ILLNESS

The following list of rules gives you a general summary of what we think is reasonable health behavior. Review them and keep the list for future reference.

1. *Awareness of What Behaviors You Can Change:* You have control over many factors that may significantly affect your health. Take advantage of the opportunity to learn how your own behavior affects your health. Strive to change your behavior in such a way as to promote your health. Learn to differentiate between those things you can change and those you must accept.

2. *Preparation for Conditioning:* Establish a relationship with a physician whom you can trust. Make sure you are able to communicate with your personal physician. Visit your physician annually in order to continually assess your health status. Do not start an exercise program without a health evaluation and advice from your doctor.

3. *Immunizations:* Be sure you are fully immunized. Diphtheria/tetanus should be received at least every 10 years. Other immunizations may be necessary under certain circumstances.

4. *Exposure:* Avoid physical, chemical, and biological hazards in the environment. This is the essence of risk reduction. Some things are obviously more hazardous than others depending on your age. The major health hazards for the 30- to 40-year-old individual are the automobile, alcohol, smoking, and weapons. There are other significant factors such as drugs, air and water pollution, and food additives that have adverse health effects, although they may be difficult to quantify.

5. *Diet:* Learn what you are eating and what you should not be eating. Food additives, such as flavor enhancers, artificial flavors, artificial colors, artificial sweeteners, and preservatives, as well as hormones and antibiotics, are chemicals. Some are known to be hazardous and others are suspect. These should be avoided. In addition, excess sweets, starches, and fats should be avoided. Your diet should contain fresh fruits and vegetables, lean meats, fish, and low-fat dairy products. Excess salt can be a problem. Obesity or overweight is a major health hazard.

6. *Drugs:* Avoid the use of drugs unless absolutely necessary. All drugs are potentially hazardous. Their benefit must be carefully weighed against their danger. Discuss this with your physician.

7. *Exercise:* Develop a regular exercise program and go through your daily activities in a way that promotes fitness. Exercise, if done regularly and under supervision, reduces the risk of hypertension and heart disease.

8. *Recreation and Relaxation:* These two are critical to your sense of well-being. They probably also prolong your life.

9. *Sleep:* When you are tired, go to sleep. Distractions such as television that keep you awake during your period of greatest evening fatigue are the single greatest cause of insomnia.

10. *Goals and Expectations:* Examine your personal expectations and the expectations which you have of others very carefully. Make sure that they are reasonable. If unreasonable, they should be changed. If you are unable to examine or change them on your own, seek help.

11. *When and How To Seek Aid:* A persistent problem deserves evaluation by your personal physician or other appropriate professionals.

ACTION PLAN FOR CHANGE

What follows is a chart that will help you to map out a strategy for changing your behavior, attitudes, and environment in ways that will reduce stressors and/or help you cope with stressors you cannot avoid.

List the changes you believe you should make to accomplish your stress management goals in order of priority. You cannot make all the changes at once. Start with the most important and/or achievable and steadily work through the list over the next *couple of years*. Pay careful attention to the pitfalls to change and the excuses you will give yourself to avoid following through with your Action Plan.

ACTION PLAN FOR CHANGE			
Changes Needed	**Target Date for Implementing Change Strategy**	**Target Date for Completing Change**	**Excuses I Will Give Myself To Avoid Making These Changes**

Changes Needed	Target Date for Implementing Change Strategy	Target Date for Completing Change	Excuses I Will Give Myself To Avoid Making These Changes

A major factor to consider when drawing up this plan is the support or hindrance offered by family, close friends, and work colleagues. It is very difficult to make significant changes on your own. Changes you make will affect other people, and they will react to these changes with support, indifference, or opposition. For example, one of many reasons why obesity is a difficult problem to overcome for many individuals is that their spouse or family may intentionally undermine the obese person's attempts to lose weight. If an obese person becomes slender and attractive, this change may be threatening to an insecure spouse who fears sexual competition. An unattractive spouse may not be appealing to others and hence does not raise the anxiety of an insecure mate. If you are serious about changing your behavior and attitudes, you need to engage the active support and help from significant people around you.

After having worked out your plan individually, certainly talk with your family members, as well as close friends and work colleagues if appropriate, about the changes you want to make. Talk about how your changing may affect them. Encourage your family members to work out action plans for themselves so that there is family support for a more healthful schedule. Make written agreements about how you will support each other's attempts to change. Schedule time to sit down and review your progress together. Commitments made openly tend to be kept better than those made quietly in your own head. The reinforcement of others actively encouraging you, changing their schedule to help you, and joining in changing with you can be enormously helpful, as well as fun. It is expected you will have to negotiate time and circumstances for implementing your plan with those whose schedules will be affected by your change in activities.

SUPPORT NETWORK HELP FOR YOUR ACTION PLAN

List the changes you plan to make in your behavior, attitudes, and environment to reduce the negative effect of stressors on you. Then list the people in your support network (see page 64). Indicate how you will ask these people to assist your efforts to change.

Change Needed	People	How I Will Ask Them To Help Me

continued

Change Needed	People	How I Will Ask Them To Help Me

IMPROVING STRESS MANAGEMENT STRATEGIES: POST-TEST

Now that you are aware of a variety of methods of increasing stress tolerance, review the two situations you gave as examples in the Pre-Test on page 123.

What could you have done differently to avoid or reduce the stress in those situations?

Situation 1 _____

_____

_____

How I felt then: _____

_____

_____

How I would try to cope now: _____

_____

_____

Situation 2 _____

_____

_____

How I felt then: _____

_____

_____

How I would try to cope now: _____

_____

_____

PITFALLS ON THE PATH TO HEALTH, OR WHY CHANGE IS DIFFICULT

Change is not always easy to implement. There are several reasons for this. You have been practicing your present style of thinking and behaving for many years. Much of your behavior and attitude has become habit. You will have trouble realizing you have engaged in the habit until after the fact. Do not make your goal the immediate and total elimination of the old behavior or the addition of new ones: You will set yourself up for failure and add to your stress. A realistic goal would be to reduce the frequency of the behavior(s) or increase the frequency of new behaviors over time so that *one or two years* from this date you can recognize substantial change. You can change habits faster by (1) asking friends to tell you when you are engaged in the old behavior; (2) deliberately engaging in the habit in an exaggerated manner several times a day so that you become supersensitized to it; and (3) keeping a log with you and writing down each time you or a friend notice the habit—reward yourself for specified reductions in the frequency of the behavior.

Often people will not change even if the present situation is not satisfactory because the discomfort of the known is not as great as their fear of the consequences of unknown behavior. If you become more assertive, for example, you will have to deal with the reactions of those around you, some of whom may prefer that you stay meek and docile. If you discover that you seem reluctant to change even though intellectually you believe you would be better off altering your life-style, then list all the consequences you can think of that would occur if you did make the specified changes. Which of these would present new problems for you? How can you decrease your fear of being different? If this problem seems to have you stymied, seek professional counseling or medical care.

Refer back to your Action Plan for Change (page 158). If the number of changes you believe you have to make is substantial, where to start and how to achieve so much may seem overwhelming. This may give you the excuse you need to avoid beginning. Do not be upset if you have found yourself with a long list of changes to make as a result of reading this workbook. Look at it as a long-range plan. Make a list of the priorities and work away at it over the next couple of years, rewarding yourself at each step. Gradual change is better for you than sudden major shifts in thought, behavior, job situations, etc.

Do not give up. You may review the material and revise your plans repeatedly without harm. Take your time and remember to enjoy yourself along the way to your goals.

A SELECTED BIBLIOGRAPHY

Adams, John D. *Improving Stress Management.* Social Change: Ideas and Applications, NTL Institute, Vol. 8, No. 4, 1978.

Altered States of Awareness: Readings from "Scientific American." W. H. Freeman, San Francisco, 1972.

Anderson, Bob. *Stretching.* Shelter Publications/Random House, New York, 1980.

Benson, Herbert. *The Mind/Body Effect.* Simon & Schuster, New York, 1979.

Benson, Herbert and Miriam Klepper. The Relaxation Response. William Morrow, New York, 1975.

Benson, Herbert and Ruane K. Peters. "Time Out From Tension." *Harvard Business Review,* Jan./Feb., 1978.

Bettelheim, B. *The Informed Heart.* Free Press of Glencoe, New York, 1960.

Blocker, William P. "Physical Activities? Teaming up Patients and Programs." *Postgraduate Medicine* 60(2): 56–61, August 1976.

Blue Cross Association. "Food and Fitness." *Blue Print for Health* 24(1), 1973.

Blue Cross Association. "Stress." *Blue Print for Health* 25(1), 1974.

Boston Women's Health Book Collective. *Our Bodies, Ourselves—A Book by and for Women,* 2nd ed. (rev.). Simon & Schuster, New York, 1976.

Brady, J. V. "Emotion and the Sensitivity of Psychoendocrine Systems." In C. C. Glass (Ed.), *Neurophysiology and Emotion.* Rockefeller University Press, New York, 1967.

Brady, J. V., R. W. Porter, D. G. Conrad, and J. W. Mason. "Avoidance Behavior and the Development of Gastroduodenal Ulcers." *Journal of the Experimental Analysis of Behavior* 1:69–73, 1958.

Cannon, W. B. "'Voodoo' Death." *American Anthropologist* 44:169–181, 1942.

Cannon, W. B. "'Voodoo' Death." *Psychosomatic Medicine* 19:182–190, 1957.

Carlson, June. *Executive Behavior: A Study of the Work Load and the Working Methods of Managing Directors.* Strombert Aktieolog, 1961.

Christen, Arden G. and Kenneth H. Cooper. "Strategic Withdrawal from Cigarette Smoking." *Ca—A Cancer Journal for Clinicians* 29(2):96–107, March/April 1979.

Coleman, Arthur and Libby Coleman. *Pregnancy, The Psychological Experience.* Bantam Books, New York, 1977.

Committee on Exercise, American Heart Association. *Exercise Training and Training of Apparently Healthy Individuals: A Handbook for Physicians.* American Heart Association, 1972.

Committee on Exercise, American Heart Association. *Exercise Training and Training of Individuals with Heart Disease or at High Risk for Its Development: A Handbook for Physicians.* American Heart Association, 1975.

Cooper, Kenneth H. *The New Aerobics.* Bantam Books, New York, 1970.

Dedmon, R. E. et al. "An Industry Health Management Program." *The Physician and Sportsmedicine* 7(11): 57–67, November 1979.

Dekker, E. and J. Goen. "Reproducible Psychogenic Attacks of Asthma." In C. F. Read, I. E. Alexander, and S. S. Tomkins (Eds.), *Psychopathology: A Source Book.* Harvard University Press, Cambridge, Mass., 1958.

DiPalmer, Joseph and Robert McMichael. "The Interaction of Vitamins with Cancer Chemotherapy." *Ca—A Cancer Journal for Clinicians* 29(5):280–286, Sept./Oct., 1979.

Doyle, Joseph T. "Type A-Type B Personality Concepts and Cardiovascular Risks." *Practical Cardiology* 5(8):27–31, August 1979.

Dressendorfer, Rudolph H. "Endurance Training of Recreationally Active Men." *The Physician and Sportsmedicine* 6(11):123–131, November 1978.

Drucker, Peter F. *The Effective Executive.* Harper & Row, New York, 1956.

Edwards, Betty. *Drawing on the Right Side of the Brain— A Course in Enhancing Creativity and Artistic Confidence.* J. B. Torcher, Los Angeles, 1979.

Egbert, L., G. Battit, C. Welch, and M. Bartlett. "Reduction of Postoperative Pain by Encouragement and Instruction of Patients." *New England Journal of Medicine* 270:825–827, 1964.

Eiger, Marvin S. and Sally Wendkos Olds. *The Complete Book of Breastfeeding.* Workman Publishing, New York, 1972.

Eischens, Roger R. et al. "A New Precise Guide to Running." *Behavioral Medicine* 6:14–17, June 1979.

Forbes, Rosalind. *Corporate Stress: How To Manage Stress on the Job and Make It Work for You.* Doubleday, New York, 1979.

Friedman, M. and R. F. Rosenman. "Overt Behavior Pattern in Coronary Disease." *Journal of the American Medical Association* 173:1320–1325, 1960.

Henry, James P. and Daniel L. Ely. "Emotional Stress: Physiology." *Primary Cardiology* 5(8):35–43, August 1979.

Hinkle, L. E., Jr., and N. Plummer. "Life Stress and Industrial Absenteeism." *Industrial Medicine and Surgery* 21:363–375, 1952.

Hinkle, Lawrence E. and Harold G. Wolff. "Ecologic Investigation of the Relationship Between Illness, Life Experiences, and the Social Environment." *Annals of Internal Medicine* 49(6):1373–1388, December 1958.

Hokanson, J. E. and M. Burgess. "The Effects of Three Types of Aggression on Vascular Processes." *Journal of Abnormal and Social Psychology* 64:446–449, 1962.

Holmes, Thomas H. and Minoru Masuda. "Life Change and Illness Susceptibility." *Separation and Depression,* AAAS Pub. No. 94, 161–186, 1973.

Holmes, T. Stephenson and Thomas H. Holmes. "Risk of Illness." *Continuing Education:*48–51, May 1975.

Janis, I. *Psychological Stress.* Wiley, New York, 1958.

Lakein, Alan. *How to Control Your Time and Your Life.* Peter H. Wyden, Inc., New York, 1973.

Lancaster, JoAnn. "Controlling Chronic Headache with Biofeedback." *The Female Patient* 4(2):25–29, October 1979.

Lewin, K. "Role of Depression in the Production of Illness in Pernicious Anemia." *Psychosomatic Medicine* 21:23–27, 1959.

Licht, Sidney (Ed.). *Therapeutic Exercise,* 2nd. ed. (rev.). Elizabeth Licht, 1965.

Machlowitz, Marilyn. *Workaholics.* Addison, Wesley, Reading, Mass., 1980.

MacKenzie, R. Alec. *The Time Trap.* McGraw-Hill, New York, 1975.

Margen, Sheldon and Bette Caan (Eds.). *Medical Clinics of North America: Symposium on Applied Nutrition in Clinical Medicine.* W. B. Saunders, Philadelphia, 1979.

Mascia, Michael F. "An Integrated Model of Health and Disease" (unpublished material).

McQuade, W. "What Stress Can Do to You." *Fortune,* January 1972.

Meyer, R. J. and R. J. Haggerty. "Streptococcal Infections in Families: Factors Altering Individual Susceptibility." *Pediatrics* 29:539, 1962.

Moritz, A. P. and N. Zamchech. "Sudden and Unexpected Deaths of Young Soldiers." *American Medical Association Archives of Pathology* 42:459–494, 1946.

Naughton, John P. "The Exercise Prescription." *Cardiovascular Medicine* 4(6):741–744, June 1979.

New York State Department of Health. State Sanitary Code, Chapter I, Pt. 16, "Ionizing Radiation."

Office of Cancer Communications, National Cancer Institute. *The Smoking Digest: Progress Report on a Nation Kicking the Habit.* U.S. Department of Health, Education, and Welfare, Washington, D.C., 1977.

Orbach, Susie. *Fat as a Feminist Issue.* Paddington Press, London, 1978.

Richter, C. P. "On the Phenomenon of Sudden Death in Animals and Man." *Psychosomatic Medicine* 19:191–198, 1957.

Robbins, Lewis C. and Jack H. Halls. *How to Practice Prospective Medicine.* Slaymaker Enterprises, 1970.

Rubin, R. T., R. G. Miller, R. J. Arthur, and B. R. Clark. "Differential Adrenocortical Stress Responses in Naval Aviators During Aircraft Landing Practice." *Navy Medical Neuropsychiatric Research Unit Report No. 12.* San Diego, Calif., 1969.

Samter, Max (Ed.). *Immunological Diseases,* Vols. 1 and 2, 2nd ed. Little, Brown, Boston, 1971.

Scarf, Maggie. *Unfinished Business: Pressure Points in the Lives of Women.* Doubleday, New York, 1980.

Schottenfeld, David and Joanne F. Hass. "Carcinogens in the Workplace." *Ca—A Cancer Journal for Clinicians* 29(3): 144–168, May/June 1979.

Selye, Hans. "Stress and Cardiovascular Disease." *Cardiovascular Medicine* 4:183–202, February 1979.

Selye, Hans. *Stress Without Distress.* Lippincott, Philadelphia, 1974.

Shea, Gordon F. "Cost Effective Stress Management Training: Helping to Achieve a Long-Term Payoff for Your Investment." *Training and Development Journal* July:25–33, 1980.

Smith, C. Kent et al. "Life Change and Illness Onset: Importance of Concepts for Family Physicians." *The Journal of Family Practice* 7(5): 975–981, 1978.

Smith, David, W. *Mothering Your Unborn Baby.* W. B. Saunders, Philadelphia, 1979.

Sonnenblick, Edmund H. and Michael Lesch (Eds.). *Exercise and Heart Disease.* Grune & Stratton, New York, 1977.

Sternbach, R. A. and B. Tursky. "Ethnic Differences Among Housewives in Psychophysical and Skin Potential Responses to Electric Shock." *Psychophysiology* 1:241–246, 1965.

Strauss, Richard H. (Ed.). *Sports Medicine and Physiology.* W. B. Saunders, Philadelphia, 1979.

Stuart, Richard B. and Barbara Davis. *Slim Chance in a Fat World: Behavioral Control of Obesity (Condensed ed.).* Research Press, 1972.

Tanner, Ogden and Editors of Time-Life Books. *Stress.* Time-Life Books, New York, 1976.

Upton, Arthur C. "Interview: Low-Level Radiation." *Ca—A Cancer Journal for Clinicians* 29(5):306–315, Sept./ Oct. 1979.

Watt, Bernice K. and Annabel L. Merrill. *Composition of Foods: Agriculture Handbook No. 8.* U.S. Department of Agriculture, Washington, D.C. 1963.

Zborowski, M. *People in Pain.* Jossey-Bass, San Francisco, 1969.